"I have been an active plaintiffs' lawyer for well over 40 years and having managed and run my own highly specialized plaintiffs personal injury/civil litigation firm for over 35 years. I fully understand the business end of running a successful plaintiffs' contingent fee law firm. However, it has taken me a long time to fully understand the successful strategy of financing such a firm. I know the same is true of many of my colleagues. We are a lot more interested in practicing law than running a small business.

"That is exactly why every lawyer who works on contingent-fee litigation cases must read Michael J. Swanson's new book, *How David Beats Goliath*. It is a book written by a financing expert in contingency fee litigation and there are very few people in our industry who have his expertise. This book will help you avoid the mistakes so many of us have made over the years in financing our business by using wrong and inefficient funding.

"I have to admit a bias in this recommendation. I have successfully dealt with Mike and his firm, Advocate Capital, for many years. I have strongly recommended their business in the past and continue to do so. It is one of the few plaintiff funding organizations left that can honestly, ethically, and expertly help us finance our own cases. However, whether you have worked with Advocate Capital or not, Mike Swanson's book is a must read. I give it the very highest recommendation."

J. Gary Gwilliam, Esq.
Gwilliam, Ivary, Chiosso, Cavalli & Brewer, Attorneys at Law
Oakland, California

"A must read for any plaintiffs' law firm. Mike Swanson lays out in a clear and concise manner the various avenues available for financing high stakes cases in today's ever-challenging litigation world."

Steven R. Cavalli, Esq.
Gwilliam, Ivary, Chiosso, Cavalli & Brewer, Attorneys at Law
Oakland, California

"This is a must read for any trial lawyer who wants to run a profitable law firm. Mike Swanson has taken some really complicated accounting and finance principles and broken it down to where any lawyer or person can understand them. But Mike even goes further and shows you how to apply them to your law firm. Applying the sound advice from this book will help you create a financially sound and stable law firm. I wish this was available when I opened my first law firm."

Kenneth L. Hardison, Partner
Hardison & Cochran, PLLC
Raleigh, North Carolina

"I went to law school to be a trial lawyer not an accountant. This book relieves you of the worries of cash flow so that you can practice law and not book-keeping. The insurance industry has all the money. This book tells you how to even the playing field, and provides a financial roadmap for any size law firm to successful cash flow. Read *How David Beats Goliath* and stop defense firms and insurance companies from financially and emotionally wearing us down."

David J. Hoey
Law Offices of David J. Hoey, P.C.
North Reading, MA

"I want to thank you for taking the time to write this appropriately titled book. The Trial Bar and the general public owe you a great deal of gratitude for taking what is a very complicated element of our practices and making it more easily understood. In that process, your book demonstrates a major risk faced by trial lawyers who gladly put their own assets at risk, everyday, for the people that they represent."

Cooper Knowles
Andrews, Knowles & Princenthal, LLC
Atlanta, GA

"Those who face Goliath in the courtroom know all too well the challenges faced by victims of negligence and corporate malfeasance. The deck is and always has been stacked in favor of monied interests, including the insurance industry attorneys we face in every case. Courageous contingency fee attorneys invest not only their time, but their assets, in pursuing justice on behalf of those we represent. We are often massively outspent by those we challenge. The ability to have assistance with the funding of cases is truly a game changing innovation. This book describes the real life drama faced by individuals and the attorneys who represent them. I salute Advocate Capital, and recommend this book to all practitioners who toil in the trenches on behalf of those we represent."

Robert Cartwright
The Cartwright Law Firm, Inc.
San Francisco, CA

"Mike, you have hit it on the head with this book! Our freedoms and constitution will soon be hanging by a thread if the trend continues."

Mitchell Jensen
Siegfried & Jensen, P.C.
Murray, UT

HOW DAVID BEATS GOLIATH ™

HOW DAVID BEATS GOLIATH™

ACCESS TO CAPITAL
for
CONTINGENT-FEE
LAW FIRMS

MICHAEL J. SWANSON

Published by Advantage, Charleston, South Carolina.
Member of Advantage Media Group.

ADVANTAGE is a registered trademark and the Advantage colophon is a trademark of Advantage Media Group, Inc.

How David Beats Goliath is a trademark of Wellgen Standard, LLC used under license.

Printed in the United States of America.

ISBN: 978-1-59932-250-6
LCCN: 2011913739

This publication is designed to provide accurate and authoritative information in regard to the subject matter covered. It is sold with the understanding that the publisher is not engaged in rendering legal, accounting, or other professional services. If legal advice or other expert assistance is required, the services of a competent professional person should be sought.

Advantage Media Group is proud to be a part of the Tree Neutral® program. Tree Neutral offsets the number of trees consumed in the production and printing of this book by taking proactive steps such as planting trees in direct proportion to the number of trees used to print books. To learn more about Tree Neutral, please visit www.treeneutral.com. To learn more about Advantage's commitment to being a responsible steward of the environment, please visit www.advantagefamily.com/green

Advantage Media Group is a leading publisher of business, motivation, and self-help authors. Do you have a manuscript or book idea that you would like to have considered for publication? Please visit www.amgbook.com or call 1.866.775.1696

Thank you to…

The Lord.

My wife, Tracy.

My Mom and Dad, Ken and Carol Swanson.

My business partner and friend, Dan A. Taussig.

The many friends who helped me with this book, especially Al Stoll, Dan Buttafuoco and Gary Gwilliam.

Preface

This book is written as a tool for lawyers as well as non-lawyers. It is intended to be of value and use to the financially savvy and the financially inexperienced alike. The information in the book has been organized into three main sections:

Part 1 (Chapters 1 through 4) gives background information on contingent-fee law firms, explaining the type of work that they do and the unique financial challenges they face. Part 1 concludes with a review of financial terms that are important to grasp as you continue to Part 2.

Part 2 (Chapters 5 through 16) is a review of 10 different sources of capital that are available to most contingent-fee law firms. Each capital source is described in detail so that its benefits and drawbacks, including relative cost, can be compared to alternative sources. The chapters are arranged (approximately) from the most expensive to the least expensive sources of capital, not accounting for risk abatement.

Part 3 contains specific advice and guidance for any law firm considering a capital-sourcing transaction (most likely a loan) and wraps up with suggestions for ways to maximize the financial strength and performance of any law firm or practice.

Table of Contents

INTRODUCTION   15

PART 1: BACKGROUND   19

　　Chapter One: Meet Wendy   21

　　Chapter Two: The Financial Realities of Contingent-Fee
　　Legal Work (aka Kyle Has a Problem)   27

　　Chapter Three: Cold Reality: Financial Deck
　　Stacked Against Contingent-Fee Firms   31

　　Chapter Four: Basic Financial Concepts   35

PART 2: REVIEW OF CAPITAL SOURCES   49

　　Chapter Five: Sources of Funding
　　for Contingent-Fee Law Firms   51

　　Chapter Six: The Hidden, High Costs of Fee Sharing   55

　　Chapter Seven: Contingent Lenders   63

　　Chapter Eight: Appeal Funding   67

　　Chapter Nine: Settlement Funding   71

　　Chapter Ten: Finance Company Loans   77

　　Chapter Eleven: Financing with Credit Cards   85

　　Chapter Twelve: Partners' Cash as a Funding Source   89

　　Chapter Thirteen: Vendor Financing   97

　　Chapter Fourteen: Bank Lines of Credit   101

　　Chapter Fifteen: Loan with Interest Pass-Through   107

PART 3: APPLICATION   111

　　Chapter Sixteen: About That Loan   113

　　Chapter Seventeen: Onward   119

CONCLUSION   131

INDEX   133

Introduction

David vs. Goliath

In the United States' civil court system, the typical defendant is a corporation and/or an individual who is being "backed" by an insurance company for payment of the claim. This is known as "indemnity." Insurance companies are especially cash-rich. In fact, the big challenge for insurance companies is deciding what to do with all the cash continually flowing into their coffers. On the plaintiff's side, we find the opposite scenario. In workplace injury cases, for example, the plaintiff is very often a working-class individual laboring at a physically demanding and perhaps even dangerous job—until difficult conditions or employer negligence gives rise to a serious injury. At that point, the worker is likely unable to work, and thus deprived of the marginal income he had been living on. When he goes to seek legal redress, he will likely be represented by a law firm that, while considered "wealthy" compared to the worker, is financially dwarfed by the insurance companies and corporate defendants. Moreover, time is also on the side of the corporations as well as size. The reality in our system is that an injured individual turns to a David to get his day in court against the Goliath.

Lawsuits Are Not A Bad Thing

Yes, you read that right. Law suits are NOT a bad thing. They are a civilized method of dispute resolution and are a constitutional right under the Seventh Amendment. Furthermore, there is not a "law suit crises" in this country. The number of law suits filed in the United States has declined significantly over the recent past. According to the National Center for State Courts (www.ncsc.org), tort cases in state courts declined by 25 percent between 1999 and 2008. And according to the Justice Department under George W. Bush, the number of tort cases resolved in U.S. District Courts fell by 79 percent between 1985 and 2003. (Source: "Federal Tort Trials and Verdicts, 2002-03," Bureau of Justice Statistics, 8/17/05.)

The Good That Trial Lawyers Do

Trial lawyers make the world a safer place by putting financial costs and penalties on corporations for unsafe behavior. The goal of the managers of a corporation is to maximize profits and shareholder value, especially in the case of public companies. Corporations do not have consciences and cannot be counted on to "do the right thing." The only way to steer corporate behavior is through economic means. Thanks to the efforts of trial lawyers we have safer cars, safer workplaces, safer toys, safer roads and many more benefits that would never have happened if it had been left to corporations or the (under-staffed and corporate-influenced) government. There would be far more accidents and severe injuries in a society where corporations could do business without regard to the human costs of their errors or "profits before people" inclination.

Why I Wrote This Book

Anyone who has ever attempted to write a book knows that it can be a long, painful and expensive process. So why do it? In my case there were two motivating factors—a belief in the important work that trial lawyers do and a recognition of the almost complete lack of financial or business education that most lawyers receive. So this book is an attempt to make a contribution to the success of plaintiff lawyers everywhere as they seek justice on their clients' behalf.

I have been an owner of Advocate Capital, Inc. (ACI) since August of 2000 and have also served as ACI's Chief Executive Officer and as a member of its Credit Committee during that time. As of this writing, my colleagues and I have spent every working day of the last 12-plus years evaluating the financial strength of countless contingent-fee law firms all over the United States. I have attempted to condense as much of that experience as possible into these pages. I hope this book will be useful to trial lawyers, but I also hope that it will give some insight to non-lawyers about the vitally important service that trial lawyers provide and the unique financial challenges they face every day. It's always easy to tell lawyer jokes, but if (God forbid) you ever need the services of a personal-injury or other contingent-fee lawyer; you'll learn first-hand about the indispensable role they play in our justice system. No, not all lawyers are rich. But even if some are considered wealthy by most standards, their net worth pales in comparison to the large insurance companies and corporations they do battle with every day. Hence the title: *How David Beats Goliath.*

– Mike Swanson, July, 2011

PART 1
Background

CHAPTER ONE

Meet Wendy

I begin this book with a true and deeply tragic story, about a woman I will refer to as Wendy, though that is not her actual name. Wendy is completely paralyzed from the neck down. She will be confined to a wheelchair for the remainder of her natural life and will require nursing care 24 hours a day, 7 days a week. She is just over 30 but has the mental capacity of a two-year-old child. Wendy has not always been like this. In the beginning of 2006, she was an active, happily married 26-year-old woman who worked full-time as an Assistant Branch Manager for a rental car company in central California. Wendy was born and raised in Northern California, graduated from high school in 1997 and went on to attend the University of California, where she earned a degree in accounting. Wendy loved her work, and in her free time she loved going dancing with her husband and taking shopping trips with her mom. She enjoyed perfect health and engaged in no risky behaviors. There was no reason why Wendy had to end up like this. Her catastrophic condition is the result of a dangerous and defective prescription drug, which caused the blood flowing out of her brain to clot. An important vein became blocked, and quickly Wendy's brain began to die due to a lack of oxygen—a condition known as catastrophic spastic quadriplegia.

At the time this tragedy occurred, Wendy and her husband, Sergio, had been happily married for a year and a half. They were heading out for a Valentine's Day dinner when Wendy developed a severe headache. She apologized to Sergio, saying she needed to go home and rest.

On February 15, 2006, Wendy sought out her primary care doctor. She was now dealing with plugged ears, dizziness, vomiting, headache, and neck pain. Wendy associated the ear pain with a runny nose and cough that had started the previous day. She was given some medication for her symptoms and sent home. She described her headache as the "worst headache of her life."

Late on the following evening, February 16, 2006, Wendy went to the emergency room. She complained of headache, earache, pain behind her eyes, head congestion, dizziness and vomiting. Because of the severity of her headache and dizziness, a lumbar puncture was done, and interpreted as normal. A CT scan of her head was also done, and also interpreted as normal. The emergency room doctor gave her some Vicodin for her headache and discharged her with a diagnosis of viral cephalgia (a headache caused by a virus).

That evening, Wendy's family heard her fall to the floor. When they went to help her, they found that she was having a seizure. Wendy was taken by ambulance back to the same emergency room where she had been seen earlier in the day. During the ambulance transport, her condition deteriorated rapidly and she was unconscious by the time she reached the ER.

At the hospital she was intubated with a breathing tube, and had a repeat head CT scan done. This time the CT scan was interpreted as being consistent with a blood clot in one of the large veins that drains the blood from her brain.

Wendy was then transferred to the area's regional medical center for neurological consultation. Neurology recommended an angiogram and an MRI of the brain, which again confirmed an extensive venous sinus thrombosis or massive blood clot in the brain.

Neurology placed a "bolt" pressure monitor in Wendy's skull, which showed a high intracranial pressure. Neurosurgery recommended urgent transfer to another larger hospital for removal of the brain clot.

On February 19, Wendy was transported by helicopter to a large teaching hospital on the West Coast. A brain CT scan and Venogram again confirmed she was suffering from a massive blood clot in her brain, which by now had caused irreversible brain damage and spastic quadriplegia. Tragically, Wendy would never walk again and would need round-the-clock nursing care for the rest of her life.

As horrible as this series of events were, Wendy and her family were fortunate to be able to obtain the services of one of the best trial lawyers in the country, Albert G. Stoll, Jr. He took their case without asking for any upfront payment whatsoever and during the three years that the case lasted, Attorney Stoll paid for all of the costs of the litigation, which ended up totaling $295,000! And he did this all with the full knowledge that if they did not eventually win the case, his $295,000 would be lost.

Wendy and her family were fortunate to get the best legal services available for a case like hers. Just as importantly, attorney

Albert G. Stoll, Jr. was financially savvy enough to access the capital he would need to hire the best possible expert witnesses for Wendy's case—12 experts in all. So rather than having to worry about how he was going to pay for the large expenses on Wendy's behalf (and for his other 40 clients), Albert could focus on implementing the best possible legal strategies. And even though he was doing battle with one of the largest corporations in the United States, a company with thousands of employees and billions of dollars in assets, he was able to access plenty of capital precisely because he had taken the time to learn about and implement many of the suggestions contained in this book. By keeping his financial ship in order, Attorney Stoll was able to access hundreds of thousands of dollars from one of the least expensive sources available in the marketplace. It was truly a "David vs. Goliath" scenario as Stoll and his staff of five employees took on and defeated a mega-corporation in a protracted legal fight.

In the end, the proceeds from Wendy's case were enough to provide the life-long medical care that she will need, along with a house for her and her husband to live in. Her basic needs will now be taken care of thanks to the skill and dedication of one lawyer.

Although the names have been changed, Wendy's story is true. But unfortunately, not every story ends like this one. Many, many times, cases like Wendy's are not pursued with the same vigor because the law firm involved has not taken the time to learn about and implement sound financial planning and strategies. And therefore they become limited in their ability to pursue justice on their clients' behalf. Make no mistake about it, there is a battle raging daily in our courts between the lawyers who represent victims like Wendy and the corporations and insurance companies whose objective is to pay as little as possible for their mistakes, and to delay any payment as long as possible.

CHAPTER TWO

The Financial Realities of Contingent-Fee Legal Work

(a.k.a. Kyle Has a Problem)

K yle Jeffries (not his real name), a 43-year-old Atlanta-based trial attorney, was experiencing steady growth in his personal-injury law practice. A recent advertising campaign had generated an influx of new cases, many of them quite promising. To support this increased caseload, Kyle went to his local bank to set up a line of credit. At the time he made his loan application he had $100,000 of his own after-tax cash invested in expenses for his current cases, and he expected to need an additional $100,000 in the coming year. To Kyle's disappointment, his bank offered an unsecured credit line of just $50,000. The loan officer at the bank cited a lack of tangible assets as justification for the modest size of the offer.

This is a common problem with trial law practices in that they lack property, equipment or other hard tangible assets that banks like to use as collateral. Lending institutions do not recognize outstanding reimbursable case expenses as a valid asset, nor are they good at recognizing future contingent-fee receivables as a valid asset, either. So Kyle was stuck with a lot of great cases and no clear choices for funding his future case expenses.

Whatever affects a trial lawyer's capacity to pursue cases affects his clients as well. One of Kyle's cases involved a factory worker, a single mother of three, who badly injured her hand while at work and could no longer perform her job. The small amount of disability coverage that she had from her employer ran out quickly and she was forced to go on public assistance waiting for her case to work its way through the system. Her insurance company refused to pay anything more than a pittance, so she turned to Kyle for help. Kyle was left quietly wondering how he was going to finance the litigation for her and for all of his other clients.

Although the suit was not complicated—a fairly straightforward worker's compensation case—the insurer dug in its heels. Using the standard technique in these situations, the insurance company chose to delay, obfuscate and even deny the claim, although it was clearly legitimate. There was zero intention on the insurer's part of working toward a reasonable settlement. This is surprisingly common and totally foreign to the average person who hears the insurance company propaganda on a daily basis. Insurance company marketing says "you're in good hands" or that the insurance company is "on your side." The reality is far different.

Another one of Kyle's newer clients was Paul Reed. Paul was a successful middle manager with a large corporation, also in the Atlanta area. One day on the way home from work, while Paul was sitting in traffic, a dump truck carrying gravel sped through a red light and crashed into Paul's car. The dump truck was owned by another large company with plenty of assets and insurance. The driver was found to be under the influence of alcohol and the truck's maintenance records were not kept up to date.

Paul was left paralyzed from the mid-chest down and would be confined to a wheelchair for the rest of his life. He also suffered brain damage that would prevent him from doing any sort of work to support his family. Kyle recognized that this was an extremely important and valuable case, but also knew it would probably require several years of litigation and easily cost tens of thousands of dollars to prosecute. As excited as he was to have this case and be able to seek justice on behalf of Paul, he still wondered what he was going to do to raise enough capital to maximize the award for his client.

It seldom if ever seems that financial lenders understand trial law practice or care to take the time to understand it. Kyle, through his diligence and skills, was holding a portfolio of valuable and important cases. He was focused on the reality that his clients could realize a just outcome, as long as they could avail themselves of highly competent and dedicated legal representation. That was the positive news. The downside of the situation was the high cost of bringing these cases, a burden that weighed heavily on him. Kyle was frustrated because he knew that clients like his have no chance of a fair and equitable result if they are to depend upon the good will of the insurance companies. Yet, the system seemed tilted against the plaintiff bar from a financial standpoint.

Several options went through his mind. One option was to step down from a couple of the more expensive cases. He also considered referring these cases to another more financially capable law firm, but of course that would dramatically reduce his eventual fee and also remove the satisfaction of being able to bring these cases to conclusion, because after all, he got in this business to help people, not merely to earn fees.

As Kyle sat at his desk eating a sandwich for lunch, he began to thumb through trade publications and browse a few websites looking at non-bank sources of funding. His head began to spin as he looked over the confusing terminology and jargon. It all seemed written to confuse the reader rather than make things clear. He recognized he was out of his element when it came to financial matters, but was embarrassed to admit it.

CHAPTER THREE

Cold Reality

The Financial Deck Is Stacked Against Contingent-Fee Firms

Can't Sell Stock

If Kyle were running an enterprise other than a law firm and needed to raise capital for growth, he could choose to sell stock to the public or sell shares to private investors. However, because a non-lawyer cannot be an equity partner in a law practice, or otherwise hold a profit interest in a lawsuit, law firms find themselves at a distinct disadvantage versus other small businesses that seek capital.

Opportunity Costs

Even if Kyle could fund all of his ongoing activities and his firm's future growth out of his own pocket—there is still the *opportunity cost* of having his own after-tax cash tied up in his ongoing cases for years and years. No one would take several hundred thousand dollars of after-tax cash and put it in a suitcase under the bed for 40 years, but that is exactly the situation that many, many trial lawyers are in, whether they realize it or not. They've made an interest-free loan of hundreds of thousands, if not millions of dollars to their firm, and those dollars stay tied up in their cases until they ultimately wind their practice down and retire.

And of course at retirement, the invested cash is worth a lot less than it was 20 or 30 years prior. Meanwhile they've missed out on the opportunity of using it to do something else, such as hire more attorneys, take on more cases and help more plaintiffs.

Afraid of Being Called Greedy

In some sense, trial lawyers' lack of attention to financial matters is understandable. They are routinely charged with the sin of avarice by their political adversaries and by most of the media. The antipathy toward trial lawyers in the U.S. is driven by hired-gun public relations firms, by the national Chamber of Commerce and of course by insurance companies. This chorus of voices habitually blames trial lawyers for any number of society's ills, such as high insurance rates, medical malpractice abuse and clogged court dockets. Contingent-fee lawyers, as a result, are hesitant to focus on financial matters. Naturally, they are sensitive to charges of being "in it for the money." They want to be thought of as what they are, professionals who come to work every day with the goal of helping their clients get fair treatment under the law. The fact is that large cases never settle quickly. They require long protracted battles. And even if the lawyer eventually earns a sizable fee, it normally has taken years to get to that result. And during that long battle, you can be assured that the law firm staff does not work on a contingency basis. No, the weekly payroll must be met, rent must be paid, and all other expenses must be kept current even during protracted cases.

Thin Balance Sheets

I have studied thousands of balance sheets of small law firms over the years. It's something I do every day. What I notice about law firm balance sheets is that they're very short on assets. Most law firms do not own much in the way of assets, whether in the form of cash or equipment or other property. A typical balance sheet shows a little bit of cash along with outstanding case expenses that are due to be reimbursed to the firm. So, the asset side of the ledger is very light.

On the liability side, there is typically some line of credit with a bank. Those entries are usually smallish amounts, because in order to do any significant borrowing from a bank, you need to show some sort of assets as collateral. The net worth of a contingent-fee law firm is typically very small, close to zero, and in some cases it's negative.

Typically the firm leases its office space, rather than owning it. They often lease their office equipment, and they may even lease their furniture. If they have invested in quality furniture, that expense may have seemed significant at the time of purchase, but furniture depreciates very rapidly.

Now when the contingent-fee firms attempt to secure traditional financing, a bank will typically say, "To get started, show us a list of assets that we can put a lien on." But of course the list the firm produces is pretty short and not very valuable in the eyes of the lender. At that point, the lender might say, "Let's just put a lien on your house or on some other non-business-related asset because your business does not have much of anything on its balance sheet."

Now this is generally true of any small service business, whether it's a small accounting firm or a tech specialist who works on computers—any service provider like that. A professional rendering personal service will typically hold a fairly weak list of assets that are available as collateral for traditional bank financing. So, contingent-fee firms are, in fact, similar to any small service business in that they typically lack tangible assets on the balance sheet. But there is one important difference with regard to Accounts Receivable.

Accounts Receivable (or Are They?)

Contingent-fee law firms have one significant disadvantage compared to other service businesses when trying to use their accounts receivable as collateral for a loan. Most service businesses (and of course manufacturers) have what a bank recognizes as "accounts receivable," which are normally in the form of invoices for work that that business has performed, but for which the business has not been paid. They've done work for their customers, they've sent out an invoice, and they can aggregate those invoices together, show them to the bank and say "Here is work I've done, contracts I have fulfilled, and here are the sums owed to me by my customers."

Banks and factoring companies understand this concept and are able to view these "receivables" as a valuable asset that can serve as collateral for a loan or can be bought at a discount (factored). What is Factoring?

If a manufacturer of ironing boards receives an order from a retailer for 5,000 boards, they will manufacture them, ship them and then print and send an invoice that says that the retailer owes the manufacturer a certain amount for the ironing boards, let's say $50,000. The manufacturer could then take that invoice and sell it to a factoring company at a discount in order to get immediate cash in exchange for a lower total payment than the original invoice. They might be willing to sell that invoice for $40,000 rather than having to wait to be paid by the retailer at some later date. The factoring company would eventually be paid the full $50,000 directly by the retailer, yielding a gross profit of $10,000 by being willing and able to wait a period of time for payment.

The problem for a contingent-fee law practice is that it does not have what is normally viewed by lenders as a valid list of accounts receivable because they don't bill by the hour and they don't regularly send out invoices. Of course the contingent-fee firm is not really owed any fees or reimbursable expenses until each case is successfully concluded. Therefore their entire inventory of cases in process is viewed as having little or no value to most lenders.

This is a source of great frustration for contingent-fee attorneys, especially the first few times that they attempt to secure traditional financing. When they meet with a lender and the lender says, "Let's see your list of accounts receivable, the attorney will typically say: Let me tell you about my cases." They will then open a file and say "This particular case is worth, realistically, $1,000,000 and my fee will be $300,000, although it may take several years to come in." Legitimately, the lawyer will also point to the track record of the law firm over several years. He will say: "Here's what I've done in the past, and here's what we project to do in the future." But what traditional lenders want is collateral. They don't want to back a business plan. They want a clear method of recourse in the case of a potential default on the loan. They're looking for buildings, land, merchandise inventories, a fleet of vehicles—something they can take as repayment on the principal of their loan if things don't go well. That's how traditional lenders work. They're not willing to offer financing based upon a business plan or fees that may eventually be owed on cases, regardless of the track record of a law firm. When money is fronted based on a business plan or projected earnings, that's usually classi-fied as equity capital or risk capital, and that's much more expensive than a loan because of the perceived risk.

From a technical standpoint, future fees on contingent-fees cases and the reimbursable case expenses from those cases are not really "accounts receivable" in the traditional sense because an account receivable is something that's owed *today*. In a contingent-fee case, no moneys are owed today. Fees will be owed in the future, most likely, especially if you have the strength of large numbers. If a firm has hundreds or even thousands of cases, one can statistically predict what those cases will be worth and when. But still, on that particular day, if the bank were to foreclose, there are no current "accounts receivable" (assets) because an asset is something of value that is owned by you or owed to you, and nothing is owed yet because the cases haven't concluded.

In the back of their minds, bankers always contemplate the end game, and rightly so. In the case of a defaulted loan, a bank can't take over a law practice and they wouldn't know what to do with the firm's cases. Banks know how to repossess and dispose of traditional collateral, such as real estate, inventory and accounts receivable, but they do not have the expertise or staffing to be able to liquidate con-tingent-fee cases. They're able to take a house, put it on the market, sell it, and keep the difference. Or to take the accounts receivable of the typical services company and collect them over the next 30 to 60 days, but they can't take over active lawsuits. So, it's a double whammy for contingent-fee law practices. They don't usually have much in the way of physical assets and they don't really have any accounts-receivable assets that a traditional lender would recognize as such.

Case Expenses Are Loans

From double whammy, let's move up to a triple whammy, which is what we get when we look at how the Internal Revenue Service views case expenses advanced by a law firm for a contingent-fee case.

The term "case expenses" (for the benefit of my non-lawyer readers) refers to the various costs incurred during the life of a contingent-fee case. This can be any costs directly related to a case, but does not normally include law firm general expenses like salaries, rent and utilities. Typical case expenses include: medical records fees, transcription fees, travel costs, deposition costs, courtroom visual aids, expert witness fees, etc. Any expenses that are necessary for proceeding with a particular case are "case expenses."

In most jurisdictions, the individual plaintiff in each case is responsible for paying these expenses and this responsibility is normally stated clearly in the attorney-client agreement. Although there is no legal or ethical requirement for a law firm to provide payment for case expenses, law firms have traditionally paid expenses during the course of a case, with the contractual agreement that they will be reimbursed for those expenses if the case is successful. This tradition developed because the law firm is usually in a better position to be able to advance the monies for case expenses than the client, who may well be injured and out of work.

Now back to the IRS' view of case expenses. It is no small irony that although banks don't typically recognize reimbursable case expenses as an asset (account receivable), the IRS takes the exact opposite view! (see PLR 8246013 – IRC Sec(s). 162, 6/30/1982). A contingent-fee firm is successful in recovering the monies it advances for case expenses most of the time. Therefore, the IRS has come to view those advances as loans rather than expenses (Ibid). The position is that it's been demonstrated over time that these cases' expenses and, of course the fees as well, are predictably going to be reimbursed/paid in large part to the firm.

So not only is the fee going to be paid—the track record says that it will—but also the case expenses are statistically likely to be reimbursed as well. And therefore, these aren't truly *expenses* and should not be taken as tax deductions against current income! Rather, the case expenses should be treated as *loans*—that's the thinking of the U.S. Treasury. The tax man believes that case expenses should be booked on a law firm balance sheet as an asset that's owed to the firm, but banks won't typically recognize these assets as having value! Of course these two groups have different motivations for assessing case expenses as they do. The banks are skittish about this money and are turned off by its "contingent" nature, while the IRS sees eventual repayment as a lock. Naturally, the IRS isn't assessing risk—their expectation of the money coming back is a mere matter of wishing to maximize tax receipts.

Let's contrast these conditions experienced by the plaintiff with the defense side of the aisle for a moment. When a corporate defendant or insurance company pays their attorneys' fees and case expenses, they are able to *immediately* deduct them from income, thereby receiving a tax advantage over the plaintiff before the case is even concluded. And insurance companies get paid in *advance* by their customers (insurance premiums) whereas contingent-fee firms (the little guys) only get paid *after* they have successfully rendered services and they *cannot* deduct their expenses against current income. Not exactly a level playing field!

So where does the cash to pay case expenses come from? Since banks are not usually very helpful, it most often comes from the law firm's after-tax receipts. The firm wins cases, earns fees, pays overhead, pays salaries, pays expenses, pays taxes and then essentially loans it back to their firm (according to the IRS) at a zero percent interest rate with no loan documents and for an indefinite time period. In fact, because there are always cases in various stages of development, although the exact balance will fluctuate over time, the law firm partners never really get back the loan they have made until they eventually retire and wind down there practices. So because of this "triple whammy," the tradition has been that the partners of the contingent-fee law firms in this country (who represent the working-class citizen) have had little other option but to lend their after-tax cash back to their firm at zero percent with no end in sight, while the insurance companies are awash in cash and get to deduct it from income when they spend it.

There have been efforts made to bring this unfairness to light and get that part of the tax code overturned. However, this campaign has been underway for years at the federal level and there hasn't been much progress. How many politicians are willing to champion a cause that will instantly be demonized as "giving tax breaks to greedy lawyers?" But remember who is at the real disadvantage. It is the plaintiff—the injured citizen, often a person of modest means.

Can't Charge Interest on Case Expenses

To make matters even worse (yes, there's more), the traditional profit on loan-making, i.e., an interest payment, is not available to the contingent-fee law firm. In most states, law firms cannot charge interest to their clients for case expenses. To do so would make the law firm a consumer lender and could make them subject to the host of regulations regarding lending to consumers. So, the lawyer or the law firm has made an interest-free loan to their client/law firm.

Note: Although most states do not permit a law firm to charge interest on case expenses they have advanced, most states *do* permit the law firm to pass through interest from a third-party lender if the borrowing was done for case expenses and if the interest was precisely calculated on a case-by-case basis.

No Outside Investors Allowed

In the United States, a non-lawyer cannot benefit from the proceeds of a lawsuit. When that principle is breached it is called *champerty and maintenance.* In other words, you cannot, as an individual, invest in a lawsuit. Thus, lawyers can't sell shares in their cases (or law firms) or create profit-sharing agreements with an investor, although it is permitted in some countries, that sort of arrangement is prohibited in all 50 states of the U.S. But guess what, you sure can invest in an insurance company or other corporation! The access to outside (non-lawyer) investors is yet another financial disadvantage endured by contingent-fee law firms vs. corporations.

Summary of Challenges: To survey the damage, so to speak, contingent-fee firms have the deck stacked against them in the area of capital access and the mechanics and treatment of their operating cash flow. They can't sell stock, though their legal adversaries certainly can. They can't enter into profit-sharing with non-lawyers, but their competition can. They don't, in the eyes of lenders, possess much in the way of tangible assets, which is not unique to service busi-nesses, but what is unique is they don't even have technical "accounts receivable" that a bank would recognize. And that portfolio of active cases, all those expenses they incur that a normal business (including insurance companies) would be able to write off as a tax deduction that year, well, the IRS says: "No, you're going to get reimbursed for most of that, so you have to book it as a loan."

All is not lost! But what is important for every contingent-fee law firm to have is a comprehensive, strategic plan to help compensate for the many inherent disadvantages that they endure. The obstacles outlined above heighten the importance of contingent-fee law firms spending time on and giving thought to their capital structure. Ultimately, their clients are depending upon them for more than just good legal advice. They need a well capitalized law firm that is in a financial position to get the best possible result in the courtroom.

Lessons on Case Expenses from Grisham and Travolta

The plight of the under-capitalized personal injury lawyer has made its way into popular culture through books such as John Grisham's *The Appeal*, which depicts the plight of a mom-and-pop personal-injury law firm that is undercapitalized and suffers through much travail. In the end (note: spoiler alert on the novel's plot) the firm ends up as a David that is unable to slay Goliaths, mainly because of financial strains. Don't be that David! Get your financial house in order, for the benefit of your clients.

A rather infamous real-life case of a similar theme was documented in the book *A Civil Action* by Jonathan Harr. The book later became the basis for a film of the same name in which real-life lawyer Jan Schlictmann was portrayed by John Travolta. The film tells the story of how Schlictmann pursued an enormous and very admirable toxic tort case in the Northeast. Unfortunately the overwhelming expenses in that case ended up bankrupting him.

The attorneys I speak to and consult with have read these books or seen these movies. They know one thing: They want to avoid a fate similar to that of the characters in these stories. However, they often lack the technical and strategic know-how to capitalize their law firms in a manner that doesn't put everything at risk and doesn't block them from opportunities to help their clients and grow their practices.

CHAPTER FOUR

Basic Concepts

B efore we begin a fairly detailed review of forms of capital available to contingent-fee law firms, it may help to review some basic financial terms and concepts.

Capital

In the presentations I make to attorneys I often start by simply asking, "Who knows what capital is?" And usually, there's a loud silence. Maybe one person in the back will say, "Money." They may think it's a throwaway answer, but they're correct. It is indeed money—available money. That's very simply what capital is. It can come from various sources, but capital is one of the key tools needed to operate and grow any business or law practice.

Asset

An asset is something you or your law firm owns that has value. This can be a piece of equipment, a vehicle, a building or perhaps a parcel of land. It can be future fees or outstanding fees that are owed to the firm. In business parlance, accounts receivable. Assets also include cash deposits, cash on hand, loans that are owed to the law firm or its partners and reimbursable case expenses that the firm has advanced on its cases.

Liability

Very simply, a liability is anything that you or your law firm owes. It can be any kind of unpaid bills, or rent that's owed, any debts you have accrued, any taxes that must be paid. In short, it's anything that is owed to another entity.

Balance Sheet

Assets and liabilities are the basic ingredients of a balance sheet—that classic accounting tool that shows everything you own minus everything you owe. Hopefully, what's left after that is a positive number, because that's your net worth. Think of the balance sheet as a snapshot in time of the net worth of a person or law firm. It's stamped with a specific date, and, again, shows everything that is owned (assets) minus everything that is owed (liabilities). What's left over is called the owner's equity or the net worth, which could be negative or positive.

Income Statement (*a.k.a.* Profit and Loss Statement or P&L)

The other document expressing business performance, for a law firm or any enterprise, is an income statement, which covers a stated period of time. An income statement might cover the activities of a full year, generally matching the calendar year. It might also cover a one-month period of time, or a business quarter—three months. An income statement shows all of the fees and other receivables that the firm has collected. Likewise, it will show all of the expenses incurred during that time, whether that be rent, telephone expenses, courier service, salaries, taxes, insurance and so on. Ideally, after all the expenses are paid out, there is a positive number at the end, which we call profit.

Opportunity Cost

As I lay out this material in conference calls and in group presentations, I put special emphasis on the topic of *opportunity* costs, because this concept is not often considered by lawyers when considering capital options. Simply, an opportunity cost is the cost of *not* doing something. Let's take the example of a contingent-fee lawyer who ties up $500,000 of his own after-tax cash in his firm's cases for the life of the firm, let's say 40 years. What is the opportunity cost of tying up $500,000 for 40 years with no interest being paid? The answer is different for everyone, because no two law firms would likely invest those funds the same way if given the chance. It's hard to put an exact number on it, but let's try to make an estimation. If you were able to get that $500,000 back out of your firm at a cost of 3 percent, and then reinvest it somewhere (maybe in your firm?) at a higher rate of say, 6 percent, the net yield of 3 percent (6-3=3) compounded annually for 40 years would result in an ending balance of $903,056. The opportunity cost of not making the above restructuring could then be estimated as $903,056 minus $500,000, which is $403,056! (before taxes). Weighing the opportunity costs of a law firm's capital structure helps give a more complete picture of the impact of various strategies that are deployed.

Time Value of Money

It's a similar situation with our next concept, the *time value of money.* In most modern economies today, the central banks are consistently increasing the money supply over time. The U.S. is no different. It has been increasing its money supply along with the rest of the world for many years. As a result, the value of a dollar today is predictably much higher than the value of that same dollar 10 years from now because the money supply is increasing at a rate that is faster than the growth of actual goods and services in production each year.

This is why candy bars that cost a nickel forty years ago now cost one dollar. Relative costs can and do change, but overall, the cost of almost everything we buy has increased in nominal terms over time because there are more dollars chasing (relatively) fewer goods.

So what does this mean for law firm capitalization strategies? Go back to the example above of a law firm leaving $500,000 of the owners' after-tax cash tied up in case expenses for 40 years. Intuitively, you know it would be better to get your hands on that $500,000 now so you can invest it (and minimize your opportunity costs) but you can actually estimate what the time value of money does to that $500,000 if it is left alone for 40 years. If we assume an annual inflation rate of only 2.5 percent, in 40 years that $500,000 will only be worth $271, 897 in present-day purchasing power. You can see how the time value of money can work against a law firm over time if the partners are not careful about planning for the long term.

UCC (Uniform Commercial Code filing)

The initials UCC stand for "Uniform Commercial Code." It's a term typically used to describe the perfection of a lien or security interest that's been granted in personal property.

When a loan is made to a business, a security interest in some type of collateral is typically granted by the debtor to the lender. Let's say the collateral is a piece of equipment owned outright by the borrower. The lender will make a public record of the security agreement by filing a UCC financing statement with the Secretary of State in the state where the debtor resides. This is referred to as "perfecting" the security interest that was granted by the debtor in the executed loan document. There is only one piece of equipment, and the borrower has pledged it. The function of the UCC is to provide public notice to other potential lenders that the collateral has already been pledged, and to sort out which of multiple lenders has "priority" by showing the time sequence of filings. It prevents the situation in which multiple lenders all accept the same asset as collateral thinking that they are in first position. By doing a UCC search on the potential borrower they will know that the asset has already been encumbered.

The Top 12 Financial Mistakes Law Firms Make

1. Failure to monitor and maximize credit scores.

2. Failure to get independent advice from a financial professional when considering financing alternatives.

3. Promoting the receptionist to CFO.

4. Financing short-term benefits with long-term debt.

5. Failure to know how much the law firm has invested in case expenses at any given time.

6. Borrowing too much money relative to law firm revenues.

7. Failure to maintain a cash cushion for slow months.

8. Failure to pay off credit cards each month.

9. Failure to read and understand loan documents and other contracts.

10. Failure to regularly review and evaluate the law firm's income statement and balance sheet.

11. Failure to understand how fixed fees can impact effective annual interest rates.

12. Accounting for case expenses improperly on the law firm financial statements. (The IRS considers them to be loans, not expenses.)

PART 2
Review of Capital Sources

CHAPTER FIVE

Sources of Capital for Contingent-Fee Law Firms

The lack of clarity among trial lawyers regarding the variety of capital sources available on the market is one of the reasons I wrote this book. Having worked in the law firm finance industry since 2000, and having recognized the confusion over the various forms of capital available to personal injury law firms, I felt it would be of value to gather this information accurately in one place. In the next 10 chapters, I will attempt to map out, as clearly as possible, the various sources of capital that are available to contingent-fee law firms.

In my presentations before groups of lawyers and in daily one-on-one consultations, I find two consistent themes. One is a lack of understanding of what capital is, where it can be obtained and what the net costs are to a law firm. The other, closely related, is a lack of appreciation of the inherent risks that certain forms and sources of capital can pose for the lawyers themselves and for their ability to achieve justice on their clients' behalf.

Most contingent-fee attorneys go into their line of work because they enjoy helping others and making a difference in peoples' lives. Unfortunately, law schools do not provide the financial and business training that is so desperately needed in any small service business, which is what a contingent-fee law firm is. To make things worse, as a small practice grows to a medium practice, very often the receptionist takes a couple of classes in QuickBooks and becomes the bookkeeper, but is unprepared and under-trained to help the law firm navigate complex financial matters. One might suggest that the law firm's CPA or accountants could provide this service. In reality, it doesn't happen. Accountants are hired simply to file the firm's taxes each year and thus are underutilized by the firm in terms of strategic financial planning in capital management. A passion for justice is the principal motivator for these law firms, causing them to put off financial planning until trouble or even a crisis arises.

Lenders that specialize in providing capital to law firms do exist, and much of what Part 2 and 3 of this book cover is the challenge of working with them successfully.

The sources of capital for contingent-fee laws firms are:

1. Fee Sharing

2. Contingent Lenders

3. Appeal Funding

4. Settlement Funding

5. Finance Company Loans

6. Credit Cards

7. Partner's Cash

8. Vendor Financing

9. Bank Line of Credit

10. Loans with Interest Pass-through

A chapter on each of these options is what follows. The chapters are organized (approximately) from the most to the least expensive as of this writing, based upon current observations. The cost ranking does not account for risk-abatement benefits, which are hard to quantify. Risk abatement will be discussed in the appropriate chapters. In reviewing the 10 sources described below, I'll attempt to explain the cost, especially the net cost, along with the pros and the cons of each form. I'll explain what type of law firm might benefit the most from that particular form of capital or which law firm situation might best apply to that type of capital.

Choosing the wrong form of capital to access can affect a law firm's bottom line, its ability to pursue justice on behalf of its clients and its prospects for growing the practice. There are even circumstances in which a poor decision on financial matters can cause a practice to be put out of business. So let's get started…

CHAPTER SIX

The Hidden, High Costs of Fee Sharing

O f all the capital sources listed at the end of Chapter 5, which would you say in is the most expensive? Generally speaking, the most costly capital source is often fee sharing (if the fee sharing is done solely for economic reasons). Not many lawyers I consult with or make presentations to would guess this, but it truly is the option with the worst arithmetic for the lawyer or firm accessing it. The reason fee sharing isn't identified as the financial loser it is by lawyers I speak to is because, frankly, it's popular. And, given human nature, we tend to look at the choices we make most often and deem them to be the soundest choices. Lots of lawyers who try injury cases or malpractice cases err on the side of using their own cash or splitting their fee revenue with other law firms in order to get access to cash to support the case work.

What I would call "pure" fee sharing is the culprit here. By that I mean, when fee sharing done strictly for the financial aspect of managing the case and not also for legal work to be done on the part of the firm that's being brought in. The collateral on fee sharing is typically going to be the individual case or cases in question and the resulting fees and cost reimbursements. The typical fee-sharing agreement is a handshake deal. If anything, there might be a one- or two-page letter of agreement on how to split the fees on the case, or cases, in question.

Surprisingly to some, the effective annual interest rate for fee sharing, as we'll see in just a moment, can be 50 to 150 percent per year! Now, there are definitely some positive aspects about using fee sharing. One of the positives is that there is little or no financial underwriting on the law firm that is receiving or benefiting from the other law firm's cash.

In other words, the partners in the law firm that will be receiving fees in exchange for helping finance the case typically will not do underwriting on the other law firm. They're not going to have them fill out an application, they're not going to check their credit, and they're not going to look at their financial statements because they're looking for payment out of the case, not out of the other firm's overall business. Therefore, a lawyer or law firm that has bad credit, but a good, strong case, can probably get another firm to fee-share on it in exchange for cash up front covering case expenses, whereas most other forms of capital may not be accessible due to a low credit rating.

Another benefit of fee sharing can be risk-abatement. Depending upon the type of agreement reached, the firm that is providing the financing may be doing so on a non-recourse basis such that if the case is lost, the reimbursable case expenses don't come back, so the law firm that put the money up realizes the loss instead of the original law firm that got the benefit of the money.

Also, with fee-sharing there will not normally be any monthly interest payments attached to this kind of financing, for obvious reasons. The firms agree to split the fee at the end of the case. So it's cash flow-neutral to the firm receiving the financing. Size of the capital amount is also relevant. The firm that has secured financing by agreeing to share fees can sometimes get access to a relatively large sum of capital—beyond what they could get via other types of financing. This is because other types of financing may be more dependent on factors like credit score, tangible assets and track record.

Yet another benefit of fee-share agreements is that UCCs are seldom if ever filed on any collateral. It's normally going to be a handshake or a side-letter agreement. Within the profession, there always seems to be that attorney-to-attorney comfort factor—a natural trust and respect that underlies these arrangements. Keeping it between attorneys, rather than having to go outside the attorney-to-attorney network for capital, is a preferred path.

Sometimes, the deep-pocketed firm that is brought in to fund the case and share the fee will contribute legal expertise and perhaps the labors of its support staff. This is clearly another positive factor for the smaller firm. They are not just getting access to capital for case expenses, but are also getting access to the larger firm's human resources and legal expertise. All of the above factors should be weighed in your evaluation a fee-sharing transaction.

We've covered some of the potential positives associated with fee sharing. The biggest potential negative, however can be the actual cost. Here is an example of how this form of case-expense funding often works out.

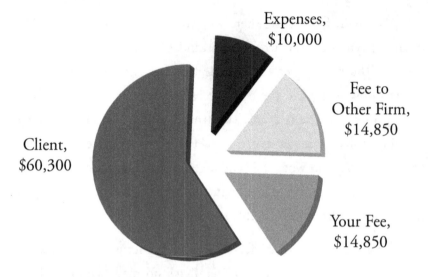

Given:

- $100,000 case (total settlement or award)

- $10,000 in expenses

- 33 percent contingent fee

- All expense dollars advanced by other firm

- 50/50 split on resulting fees

- Case length = 12 months

- Fee split is purely financial (no services provided)

As shown, here is a case that will be worth $100,000 at settlement (or award). There are $10,000 of expenses in the case with a $29,700 contingent fee ($14,850 + $14,850), and all the expenses are advanced by another firm in exchange for a 50-50 split on the resulting fees. The case is assumed to last for one year and it is likewise assumed that the fee split is purely financial—no services augmenting it. Lastly, this calculation does not factor in any benefit from risk abatement if the firm providing the financing is doing so on a non-recourse basis. All that being said, one can see from the chart, that the smaller firm is getting the use of $10,000 to cover case expenses for a year. Now then, what are they paying for that? They pay half of their $29,700 fee. So they're effectively paying $14,850 in exchange for using the other firm's $10,000 for one year. Therefore the effective annual interest rate in this example is 148.5 percent! ($14,850/$10,000 = 148.5%)

Not only is that a very high effective rate, but the logistics of the case actually make the effective rate even higher because the $10,000 of expenses would not be paid out on day one of the case. More likely, they would be paid out as needed on the case over time. So the larger firm would not be putting up $10,000 on day one. They would pay the expenses as they go, working toward a $10,000 total at the conclusion of the case.

For the smaller firm, which in reality is not getting access to $10,000 for a full year, the effective annual interest rate runs notably higher than 148.5 percent. Why didn't the smaller, less-capitalized firm negotiate a better deal? The answer, in part, is that things have always been done this way. The mindset of the partners in the small firm goes like this: "We earned a fee of $14,850 and we didn't have to put up any money." And the larger firm, to defend its 148-plus percent interest rate, can at least note the fact that it incurred risk. If the case was a loser they would be out the dollars they advanced. That risk notwithstanding, the larger firms often advance funds on a fee-sharing agreement quite willingly. You can't blame them. If you're a lawyer with capital and you're approached by a smaller firm that you trust to pursue the case they're presenting to you, that's a pretty good return on your capital!

The smaller firm is unlikely to even think about the effective annual rate it is paying. Even if the case took two years instead of one, the effective annual interest rate is almost 75 percent. And people complain that credit cards are expensive! I tell the lawyers I speak with that they need to re-examine their fee-sharing agreements and view them under the broad category of capital acquisition. In other words, don't see it as just a cooperative tradition; put a pencil to the actual numbers. It would make sense at the end of every case that you fee-shared just to do a simple calculation. How much capital did the other firm put up, for how long and what did you give up in exchange for that?

Here's a good formula to use:

Amount of Fee Paid to the Other Firm

divided by

Amount of Capital Advanced by the Other Firm

divided by

Number of Months the Capital Was Advanced

multiplied by 12

This will give you the effective annual interest rate you paid. As a straightforward interest calculation, it is undeniably high. However, there may be extenuating factors. Your feeling about the high rate will surely be mitigated if the funding was done on a non-recourse basis, or if you got access to the other firm's expertise or personnel. In the end there is a judgment to be made, but it is important to be fully informed about each fee-sharing transaction and be aware that there may be more economical sources of capital available to your firm.

Important Note on Fee-Sharing

The discussion of fee sharing thus far has focused primarily on the financial impact of giving up 50 percent of your future fees for access to capital for case expenses, since access to capital is the primary topic of this book. However, as in every case, the best interests of the client must come first. Often times it is actually in the client's best interest for the initial law firm to bring in a second firm via fee sharing. Not only for capital reasons, but for reasons of expertise and experience. When two firms come together and contribute legal and financial resources to a case, the client is kind of getting two law firms for the price of one, since the overall fee to the client is unaffected. The (potential) additional expertise, experience and overhead that the second (usually larger) firm brings to the table must be considered as a positive for the client. And of course the client comes first.

CHAPTER SEVEN

Contingent Law Firm Funding

C ontingent law firm funding is a process whereby a funding company agrees to purchase a portion of a law firm's future fees on a case or group of cases that are not yet settled. The case or cases may not even have been filed in the courts yet. Typically, the funding company will carefully evaluate the expected case value using its own legal counsel and will attempt to judge the odds of a success, along with the anticipated timing of a payout. If it believes the case has a strong chance of succeeding, it may offer to purchase a portion of the fees that the law firm is expected to earn, but usually no more than 50 percent of the expected fees so that the law firm will remain sufficiently motivated to pursue the case vigorously.

For example, if a case is expected to generate $500,000 in fees , a contingent funding company may offer to purchase up to $250,000 of those expected future fees. The price that the funding company would be willing to pay depends upon the perceived odds of success and expected timing, but the rule of thumb seems to call for a 50 percent discount if the payout is expected within a year or so. In the example above, that would result in an offer of $125,000 to purchase $250,000 of future fees. If the case took 12 months to pay out, that would result in an effective annual interest rate of about 100 percent. That's pretty pricey on its face, but it is important to note that in addition to the cash payment by the funding company, there is also a risk-abatement benefit to the law firm in that if the case is lost, there will be no repayment required of the law firm. Thus, using contingent funding can enable the law firm to "take some chips off of the table" earlier in a case, although the effective annual rate for doing so is quite high compared to other forms of capital.

Underwriting for contingent law firm funding is usually much less rigorous than for bank financing or other more common forms of recourse lending, so law firms that have bad credit may find this to be an available option if they have been shut out of other sources of capital. The underwriting that is done is usually confined mostly to the value of the case being funded, limiting the number of documents to be submitted by the firm. The funding company may or may not file a UCC (our experience is that they often do not), but even if they do the collateral named is normally restricted to the specific case being funded. This leaves the law firm's other cases and accounts receivable unencumbered as regards to other potential borrowing or funding.

There's normally no monthly interest payment, although that does vary from situation to situation. As with fee sharing, there can be a relatively large potential line of credit compared to what a traditional lender would provide.

Weighed against those advantages are some big negatives. One of them obviously is expense. An annualized interest rate of 75 to 100 percent is enormous. It can't be glossed over or taken lightly by the firm that is paying it. Another negative is the wild-west aspect of these transactions. You're usually dealing with non-attorneys who are in a commercial finance company that is outside of the mainstream. So you need to be very careful about getting sound financial advice or even legal advice in these transactions. It's vital that you fully understand the transaction and all the fees that might be involved. Don't fail to read the loan document carefully. Your likelihood of entering one of these agreements is minimal, a fact no one should lament. Due to the credit crisis that struck in 2008, many of these contingent lenders ceased operation.

If you do find one of these lenders still doing business, quite likely they are a diminished version of what they were. It was in fact the bigger contingent lenders that really got burned, because when it comes down to it, you can't out-lawyer the lawyer. You're not going to work the deal such that the attorney or the firm has given you just their good cases—they are going to give you the riskiest cases. And that's exactly what happened. A couple of these lenders looked like geniuses for a while. They built up their portfolios quickly and had very large sums advanced, and then without much warning they took massive losses because they tried to out-lawyer the lawyers.

CHAPTER EIGHT

Appeal Funding

You take on a plaintiff, prepare the case, bring it to trial and achieve a favorable verdict in the courtroom. And then the other side files an appeal. Just when success seems to have been obtained, further delays are added, delays often measured in years. And of course these delays have financial impact, in that fees earned by the law firm representing a plaintiff who has won a case at trial will not be paid until an appeal has been successfully defended.

In order to address the financial impact that appeals have on plaintiff law firms, there are a handful of commercial finance companies that offer a product normally referred to as appeal funding. Appeal funding is typically structured as a purchase, not a loan. When a law firm wins a case at trial for its client, it has in fact earned its fee on the case. The fee is due and payable, but the payment is subject to a successful defense of an appeal, if one exists.

Companies that offer appeal funding will purchase a portion of that earned fee from the law firm. The pricing that seems prevalent in the market at this writing is a 100 percent return for the finance company. In other words, if the finance company advances $100,000 to the law firm, they expect to get $200,000 back upon a successful defense of an appeal. This may seem like a significant return, but there is an important twist: These deals are normally offered on a contingent basis, such that if the case is eventually lost, the finance company gets nothing and experiences a $100,000 loss, plus the loss of underwriting costs, overhead, and the cost of the monies advanced. Thus, these companies need to charge prices high enough to compensate them for the very significant risks they are taking. Additionally, appeal funding companies need to have very experienced, savvy legal counsel working for them in order to successfully choose the cases that will most likely survive an appeal. Another factor when evaluating appeal funding pricing is that appeals can run for years, so that an investment of $100,000 might eventually yield a return of $100,000, but there is a risk for the finance company that it might take years to reach a final decision, effectively reducing the annualized return on investment.

Appeal funding, because of its risk-abatement component, can be an attractive alternative to a firm that has won a verdict that is being appealed. By selling a portion of the fee that is owed to them, the law firm can take chips off the table. They can mitigate some of the risk that the appeal might in fact be successful and bring about a total reversal of the verdict, thereby leaving the firm with no fees whatsoever. One of the nice things about appeal funding is that it requires very little underwriting of the law firm itself. So if the partners have bad credit, tax liens or other financial problems, appeal funding can still normally be accessed. What matters to the appeal funding provider is the strength of the case that resulted in the verdict and the likelihood that an appeal will succeed.

Not accounting for the risk-abatement impact, the average effective annual cost that we are seeing in the current market is in the range of 35 to 100 percent, assuming the appeal is concluded between one and three years. If, after weighing the pluses and minuses, you decide to pursue non-recourse appeal funding, make sure you deal with an experienced and reputable company. You should also be certain that the appeal funding provider will not be able to interfere in the attorney-client relationship or in the management of the case.

CHAPTER NINE

Settlement Funding

S ettlement funding is a transaction entered into by a law firm that has a settled case—one that has a signed settlement agreement in place but will not yield a prompt payment to the lawyer. Delay in payment will often stem from statutory requirements. It could also have even been negotiated into the settlement that the defense has an extended period—say, 90 to 180 days—to make the actual payment. For these circumstances there is a product in the marketplace that will purchase a portion of the lawyer's fees and reimbursable case expenses on that settled case. The lawyer or the law firm gives up some of the payment-in-full he would have received if he were willing to wait for his funds.

The collateral in the settlement funding transaction is typically limited to the monetary value of that individual case. It doesn't normally encumber other assets of the law firm or its partners. The effective annual interest rate on settlement funding at this time is normally between 25 and 45 percent on an annualized basis. However, most of these transactions are fairly short-lived. A one-year settlement funding deal would be considered a very long transaction in terms of the length of time that the money is out.

There are positives for this product. Like other transactions mentioned earlier, there's little or no financial underwriting done on a law firm. Again, the lender in this case is looking strictly at the strength of the obligor, the defendant who's being required to make this payment. It's normally the defendant or their insurance company. So they will underwrite the particular insurance company that may be obligated to make this payment by looking up their S&P rating. But there's little or no financial underwriting done on the law firm, itself.

There is also risk abatement because most of these transactions do not require a repayment of the principal if something outside the law firm's control occurs that would cause the settlement not to be paid. This would exclude any kind of fraud being perpetrated by the law firm. But if, for example, the obligor on the settlement agreement were to go bankrupt in the time between the settlement funding transaction and the actual payment, that normally is not the responsibility of the law firm.

As with other more expensive forms of lending, bad credit typically is not an issue in settlement funding, and there would be no credit check on the partners. Likewise, there is normally no monthly interest payment for this product, so it's cash flow-neutral. And, as might be expected, there's the potential for a relatively large line of credit or access to capital available, particularly in proportion to the credit rating or annual revenues of the law firm or its guarantors. This can be an advantage. If you opt for settlement funding, you can expect to grant a security interest and have a UCC filed, but it's typically filed only on one case, not on all assets of the firm. So again, it leaves other assets available to be encumbered, if necessary, for additional leverage or borrowing.

There are definite negatives to settlement funding. It's still very expensive compared to other forms of financing, as we'll see. An annualized interest rate of 25 to 45 percent is nothing to sneeze at—that's a very high rate to be paying.

What surprises me is seeing law practices with abundant cash on hand participating in settlement funding. From a financial-analysis standpoint, firms with plenty of liquidity should never engage in this activity, though they quite often do. One of the reasons for this willingness is that they don't do the math on the actual interest rate they're paying. Not that it would be easy. The documentation from the lender tends to be so confusing that it's very difficult to calculate the effective annual interest rate. These transactions are typically structured such that there would be a certain percent owed if the full principal is repaid within 30 days. More often it works out that payments are assessed in small lump sum amounts based upon the number of days or fractions of months that the money is in use.

Again, if you're not careful about the agreement, it can result in liens on all your assets, not just that particular case. These transactions are not normally structured as loans. Instead they are structured as purchase agreements, similar to what a factoring company would arrange. A settlement funding company will agree to purchase a certain portion of future fees in exchange for a payment now and additional payments later. The additional payments they make over time go down in size depending on how long the money is out. That's why it can be so difficult to calculate the actual average interest rate. To reiterate, our experience in the marketplace after analyzing many of these types of transactions is that the annual interest rate will fall between 25 and 45 percent.

Psychology and emotions enter into this discussion, as with most discussions of money and finances. Take the Kyle Jeffries law firm, which has just won a big case. The partners win their judgment in April and they are due $600,000 that is expected to be paid in June. The Jeffries firm would contact a settlement funding group, and be given an offer. The firm would be told something along the lines of: "We'll buy $100,000 of that $600,000 from you. And all we're going to charge you is two percent a month or a fraction thereof." In that instance, the Kyle Jeffries firm would be looking at a fee of $2,000 on the $100,000 if it's paid back within the first month. Very well, let's say it is repaid in exactly one month. Based on two percent a month, the annual interest rate is 24 percent. Switch that, and the Jeffries firm repays in two weeks. That's a 48 percent annual interest rate, because Jeffries is paying $2,000 to get the use of $100,000 for two weeks.

The documents on these transactions nearly always calculate the rate "per month or a fraction thereof." So if you repay in full on day 32, you might as well have waited until day 60, because you're getting hit for $4,000.

The term "fee acceleration" is usually part of a settlement funder's marketing, to obscure the fact that it's a high-interest loan. My sense is that Kyle Jeffries or another attorney is thinking, big deal, I'm about to get $600,000. Now I'm pretty flush. I don't care about the $2,000 hit, just give me that check.

It's not a good way to run a business over a long time. And maybe the thrill of the win affects the decision-making. A great amount of hard work has led to a nice victory, and people start talking about vacations and sports cars and bonuses for the staff. This takes us back to the John Grisham novel, *The Appeal*, about that mom-and-pop firm that has every reason to think they've won a big settlement. Caught up in the excitement of apparent victory, they spend the money before they actually have it.

Best practices in law firm financing would preclude this. There is always going to be exhilaration at winning a big case, but the underlying attitude has to be: *We're running a business here.* The possible exception would be a firm that's essentially broke, but has one big settlement signed and agreed upon. They go with settlement funding, to solve a liquidity problem. They don't have to worry about getting their credit checked—they've already been rejected. They may be at the point where they have maxed out all their credit cards. That's a special situation. It should occur rarely. Yet you do find lawyers wanting an instant reward, one they are willing to overpay dramatically for, and this is simply not a fiscally logical way to run an enterprise.

Full disclosure: Our company, Advocate Capital, offers settlement funding. At least nominally we do. But we almost never do these deals—on average, we do one or two a year. Instead what happens is we get a request for it, and we ask the lawyer calling us why he's making the request. We have a dialogue with him in which we state outright what the effective annual interest rate is going to be. Then we bring up standard case-expense funding, where the effective annual interest rate is less than one percent.

So although we do make settlement funding available, we rarely engage in it because most firms that call us can have access to capital a lot cheaper with some of our other products. In particular they do far better using case-expense funding than settlement funding. So we typically turn our settlement-funding leads into case-expense clients. Often the settlement funding request is the beginning of our education process. From our standpoint, if the goal was to maximize our rate of return, we would gladly engage in settlement funding because look at the rates you can get. That's not Advocate Capital's mission. We believe in what our clients do. We know we're not helping them by maximizing the interest they pay. We're doing the opposite. Our consistent message is this: If you're going to borrow money, borrow the cheapest money you can get first. And settlement funding is in no way the cheapest money most law firms can get.

CHAPTER TEN

Finance Company Loans

Because trial law firms are so consistently underserved by traditional banks, there has always been an unmet need for capital in this sector of the legal profession. As a result, non-bank finance companies have moved in to try to serve this market and fill the breach left by the banks.

This was especially true during the early 2000s, when our economy was expanding, interest rates lowered and there was a lot of what you would call "cheap money" in the finance system. During those years, there were plenty of well-capitalized hedge funds, private equity funds and asset-based lenders who were eager to deploy assets and saw the law firm finance market as a good opportunity for fat profit margins.

Since so many startup finance companies had easy access to capital and contingent-fee law practices were bumping along with their traditional financing difficulties, a new business model was born. As the decade came to an end, however, the world-wide financial machinery broke down, markedly thinning the ranks of these finance companies that had targeted trial law practices. There are still a few of these lenders doing business, and as the general credit markets in our economy recover and more liquidity becomes available, one would expect there to be more appearing on the scene.

Because finance companies are not banks, they're generally not as closely regulated as banks tend to be. Therefore they enjoy more flexibility in the types of loans they can make, in the pricing they can set and in the terms they can choose to offer. The typical collateral of a finance company loan will be the accounts receivable of the law firm, but may extend to include all law firm assets, and sometimes even the personal assets of the law firm partners. Unlike traditional banks, finance companies who target contingent-fee law firms do a good job of understanding that these firms do have valid accounts receivable, in terms of establishing collateral.

That being said, there are a few potential positives about dealing with a non-bank finance company. One example is that it can often be easier to qualify for a loan from one of these companies than it can be from a bank. Also, they can often make a larger loan than a bank could make. And sometimes they are willing to underwrite the law firm based upon the projected value of their cases rather than just looking at historical financials, as a bank would do. Because non-bank finance companies are not as regulated as banks, they can be more creative in their underwriting.

There are finance companies that know the contingent-fee law industry quite well. These companies have specialized in lending to trial law firms and have become proficient at the underwriting. In general they've come to understand how a contingent-fee law firm operates. They are not scared off by some of the factors banks are skittish about—for instance, the mere word "contingency." There's a joke that says "a bank is a building full of people who've never done anything for the first time." When it comes to underwriting, there is a lot of truth to that. As a prospective borrower, you can make a great case to a traditional banker about the excellent risk-adjusted return he'll enjoy by lending to you, however, if you are asking him to do something he hasn't done before you may feel you're talking to a brick wall.

Knowing that banks only want to underwrite traditional, typical service businesses or manufacturers, finance companies have exploited that blind spot. For a plaintiff's attorney, this means it can be much easier to deal with a non-bank finance company than with a bank.

There are some negatives to working with non-bank finance companies. Probably the greatest negative is that their pricing is typically much higher than a bank's pricing—it can range from 15 to 25 percent per year, whereas bank rates are typically in the Prime to Prime-plus-1 percent range. Obviously this is a very high interest rate compared to many other forms of capital. Usually, the higher the rate a borrower is willing to pay, the higher the risk they represent. So many of the law firms that have been willing to pay these rates have done so because they have not had access to lower-priced capital, due to risk factors. Others have proceeded with these high-priced loans not really understanding the drag that these rates would have on their practice.

Either way, these higher-priced loans are fraught with danger for the lender because of higher risk and/or unsophisticated borrowers who manage to get themselves into situations that endanger the very life of their practice. Another negative is that the underwriting for a finance company loan can be more intensive and more time-consuming because they may do things a bank wouldn't. They may roll up their sleeves and actually study the cases the law firm has in inventory. Some of these lenders also perform on-site pre-funding audits of the potential law-firm borrower. These lenders may also require a lien on all the firm's assets – not just on the accounts receivable.

Another potential negative of a non-bank finance company loan is pricing that may be difficult to decipher and fees that are hidden or difficult to calculate. So, if these lenders do prove more flexible in looking at collateral, and show more regard for the future value of cases, you will likely pay for that flexibility in much higher pricing. It bears repeating, however, that in a world of lenders that don't understand trial lawyers, these lenders are an exception. Because they do it all day long, many have become proficient at it. Many non-bank finance companies actually employ attorneys on staff or as contractors to help them evaluate the practices they're considering making loans to.

Another potential negative with a finance company is that they have tended to come and go over time. This is because they are often financed by private equity funds or hedge funds, which are relatively volatile and less dependable sources of capital for the finance company over the long haul. This was demonstrated in the late 2000s when several of the largest non-bank finance companies in the contingent-fee market either went out of business or stopped funding loans for a period of years—with little or no notice to their clients.

So, if you are considering a transaction with a non-bank finance company, it's important to ask them about their funding sources. Start by asking them if they have ever not funded a loan request for a customer, and if so, why? Have them explain to you the capital structure of their organization. The answer will help you assess how dependable they're going to be as a lender.

Because the pricing is so high on this particular product, it's important to have a very clear business reason for borrowing at such high interest rates, and a very clear plan on how to pay the principle back. We have seen instances in which a non-bank finance company will create a relationship with a law practice that might be grossing $1 million a year and will lend them $1 million at 20-plus percent interest. Before the firm realizes it, that advertising campaign they borrowed the $1 million for is long gone, but the loan is still there, and it's eating up $200,000 of their fees per year. Payments of that magnitude create a very difficult hole to dig your way out of. If you're going to use money that's this expensive, you need a clear plan of repayment—one that will offer a very high level of certainty about the return. Think of it this way: Interest is basically the "rent" you pay to use someone else's money for a while. You're getting use of these funds for a period of time, and for the use of that money, you pay interest. Well, if you're going to pay $200,000 a year to "rent" $1 million, you need to be making at least $200,000 or more a year from your use of that $1 million, otherwise you are moving backwards. This especially applies if you are borrowing long-term in order to pay for short-term needs. For example, you would not rent an office building for a year and then move out, but continue to pay rent.

Likewise, you would not want to borrow $1 million at 20 percent per year, and then blow through that $1 million on a consumable like advertising, ending up with the loan in place and monthly payments still due indefinitely, when the use of the money is long gone.

Unfortunately, I've spoken to firms that have done just that. One attorney in Texas, for example, was grossing about $2 million a year in fees. He is an excellent lawyer and is very respected by his peers. At one point, he decided to go into a new area of practice, that being nursing home litigation. He took his business plan to a non-bank finance company and secured a loan for $2 million to conduct a marketing effort aimed at building up this area of his practice.

After borrowing that $2 million and spending it on advertising and marketing for a year, the cases he was able to secure came nowhere close to yielding fees that would enable him to pay off the $2 million loan. He abandoned this area of practice but was still saddled with the loan and the monthly interest payments and probably will be for many years.

It's always a bad idea to finance short-term benefits with expensive, long-term financing. Advertising, a valuable activity for law firms if it's paid for appropriately, is the budget item that firms tend to finance unadvisedly.

A general working capital loan priced at 15 percent to 25 percent is a very dangerous product for law firms. Firms that take out this kind of loan often find themselves financially stuck. They use the borrowed sum for general working capital or other short-term benefits, and they're stuck with long-term debt at very high prices, at which point they have nowhere else to go.

I mentioned earlier that some non-bank finance companies do specialize in loans to contingent-fee lawyers, and become quite familiar with how such firms operate. Too often, though, they don't use that familiarity to build a sound and sustainable relationship with the borrower. At the very high rates they charge, they end up with a portfolio of customers who were in a bit of a bind or not thinking very clearly when they applied for their expensive loans. Who's going to borrow money at 20 percent a year if they don't have to? Too often the answer is desperate people, or people who are not making a good business decision. The non-bank finance companies that made a lot of loans of this type have gotten into big credit problems themselves, carrying many bad loans on their books. That's because they have either knowingly lent money to law firms that really needed the money and did not have a solid business plan on how to pay it back.

The Myth of the Tax Deduction

In order to get potential borrowers to accept high interest rates, one of the techniques that non-bank finance company lenders have used is to point out to the potential borrowers that because interest is a business expense, it's tax-deductible, and therefore, it's not as expensive as it looks. I call this the myth of the tax deduction. By that reasoning, why not double the interest rate and give your law firm an even bigger tax deduction? While it is true that, most of the time, loan interest is a deductible business expense for a law firm, it does *not* follow that if a little expense is good, more expense is better.

CHAPTER ELEVEN

Financing with Credit Cards

C redit cards are more commonly used to finance contingent-fee law practices than most people would ever guess. It's especially common when a practitioner is just starting out.

Prior to the financial crisis in the late 2000s, credit cards were extremely easy to obtain and use. At that stage of the economic cycle, we all would open our mailboxes every day and often have four or five direct mail pieces from credit card companies asking us to sign up for one of their cards. So it was not at all unheard of for a trial lawyer or his practice to have four, five, six, even 10 credit cards and be using them all together as a means of financing the practice. In fact this still goes on today. We have routinely seen law firms that have $100,000 worth of outstanding credit card debt.

At this writing, credit card rates for new borrowers are ranging between 11 and 16 percent. But rates often go much higher, up to almost 30 percent if a payment is missed or is even late. Pretty good deal for the banks, don't you think? Get bailed out by the government, borrow from the Fed at under 1/2 percent and then turn around and charge your customer anywhere from 11 to 29.99 percent. But I digress.

It's a great deal if you can get in on it, but for customers of credit card companies the deal is not so good. Credit cards (just as in personal finance) can be dangerous for a law practice, because again the effective annual interest rates can be very high—figure 12 to 30 percent.

There are some potential positives about credit cards. First, there usually is no secured collateral in credit-card lending. Card accounts are set up based on the personal credit history of the individual applying for the card. That can be a benefit, because as we've noted before, law practices may have very little in the way of tangible assets that they can leverage as they go and seek capital. So the zero-collateral requirement can be considered a positive from that perspective.

Also, although credit-card lending tightened up after 2008, cards can still be fairly easy to get, especially if you have a clean credit history. They are also quite easy to use in that they are accepted for so many different types of transactions—including online transactions. Most credit card companies will even provide you with checks that you can write in order to secure cash advances or take care of your payables.

Another potential benefit to using credit cards is expense tracking. At the end of the year, a credit card company will typically provide a summary of transactions grouped by type and vendor. This information is usually also available online both monthly and at year-end. This can be a benefit to a law practice that does not have a lot of bookkeeping staffing available.

Probably the biggest negative to using credit cards to finance your law practice is the sheer cost of this form of financing. If you end up having to pay 25 to 30 percent a year for your capital, comparable to that of a finance company loan, it's unlikely that you will get a return on that capital that exceeds your cost.

Although you may get a great initial rate from a credit card, typically the rates go up after a trial period. If you are not careful and your bookkeeper is late on one payment, you can get burned by some clause hidden in the fine print of your contract. These obscure provisions often let the card company immediately bounce you up to rates approaching as high as 30 percent in some states. That's a danger with credit cards—your monthly interest rate can double overnight.

Another potential negative of credit cards is that the issuer can unilaterally lower your credit limit without giving you notice. You may think you have a $20,000 limit and if your current balance is $10,000 you will assume you have $10,000 of availability. However, without notice and without any apparent reason, the bank can decide to change your limit to $10,000. Now that $10,000 of availability you thought you had is gone! And they don't even have to inform you! To make matters worse, now your credit score will likely go down because instead of having 50 percent utilization on that card, it's now 100 percent utilization. Percent of credit utilized on credit cards is one of the variables that go into the calculation of a credit score. There was a rash of this kind of thing in the late 2000's, but it still continues today.

Be wary also of the fraud factor. Credit cards present a unique problem in that respect. As nice as it is that they're easy to use, it's also easy for someone to steal your card or steal a number, especially if you're using it online. Employee fraud or theft can also be a problem with credit cards. Bank loans don't tend to pose this type of problem. It's a lot easier for an employee to take advantage of their employer if there are company credit cards around.

Like some consumers, law firms often try to play the interest-rate musical chairs game by moving from one card to another every few months in order to access low teaser rates. The potential problem is that if the music stops in terms of access to that next credit card, the firm can end up paying a lot more interest than was expected.

One other point about credit cards should be made. Even if you make your monthly payments and use cards responsibly, too much credit card debt or simply too much credit card availability—or just the number of cards you have—will cause a negative impact on your credit score. The use of the card, how many cards you have, what your balances are, and what those balances are relative to your limits are all factors that could affect your personal credit score.

Some firms, typically in the very early stages of their formation, have been able to use credit cards for a short period of time to get their practices up and running. The smart ones switch to a less expensive form of capital as soon as they're able to. In general, maintaining a large credit card debt balance over the long haul, or keeping multiple accounts open, will cause problems.

CHAPTER TWELVE

Partners' Cash as a Funding Source

Covering case expenses and general overhead with partners' cash is by far the most common way contingent-fee law practices finance their practices. Once in a great while the partners use their own cash to finance the law practice and actually create a transaction whereby they pay themselves back some interest. However, the vast majority of the time, the partner's cash is used to finance the practice without a conscious decision being made to lend the money to the firm. As expenses come up, they're paid out of the firm's after-tax cash, which reduces the amount of salary or profits that are available to the partners as compensation.

For a successful established firm that's been practicing a number of years, the number of dollars tied up in ongoing case expenses can be very large. The total can run into the hundreds of thousands, or even millions of dollars. This happens basically as a matter of tradition. Because most plaintiffs are not able to pay ongoing case expenses, law firms have traditionally agreed to advance those expenses from the firm's capital with the agreement that the firm will be reimbursed for those expenses at the conclusion of a successful case. Very seldom will this self-funding practice be followed as a result of deliberation and a conscious decision. It's not a matter of the partners all sitting around a conference table and studying the various options and looking at pros and cons, then declaring, "Let's make an interest-free loan to our practice for an indefinite time period." It's more of a default.

There are no ethical or legal requirements for the firms to advance case expenses on behalf of their clients. It has merely been a traditional way of operating for most contingent-fee firms.

Once the process starts, it rolls on perpetually. There are always cases of all different ages in a larger firm's portfolio. As one case is settling and the case expenses are coming back to the firm, there are other cases ramping up that are requiring case expenses to be paid. Although there's some fluctuation in the amount being advanced over time, the partners' cash that's tied up in ongoing case expenses never really comes back to them completely until they wind down their law practice and retire, some day long in the future.

This practice of using partners' after-tax cash to fund case expenses has several negative effects on contingent-fee firms. One is the impact on the compensation of the partners themselves. Contrary to what most people think, the average contingent-fee lawyer is not rich, and many times is not really even a high-income producer. As the owners of a small service business, these lawyers enjoy a moderate to sometimes above-average income; however it is usually highly variable from year to year. In many practices, the partners may take a small salary, or even none at all, and are then being paid their compensation either quarterly or at the end of the year. And those compensation payments are not based upon profits, but rather on *available cash flow.*

Available cash flow is going to be roughly equal to the firm's profits minus taxes minus any new dollars tied up in case expenses. If a firm is in a growth mode it can get to the end of the year, show profits on the books that are taxable, but not have the cash to either pay the taxes or to pay themselves their compensation.

The issue of "phantom profits" tends to haunt contingent-fee firms. As the year comes to an end, the partners will look around and say, hey, we had a great year. We won a lot of cases. We helped a lot of clients. We've certainly booked a lot of fees. Then they sit down with their accountant in December and when they look in the checkbook and there's no cash there, they scratch their heads and wonder where it all went. Well, if they're growing their practice, most of it probably went into existing cases to advance case expenses. So it can be a problem on two fronts. Not only can they be stuck without the cash to make the necessary tax payments, they can also be unable to pay their year-end compensation.

A trial lawyer's money is usually located where his thoughts and his passions are located—in his cases. I've never met a trial lawyer who didn't love to talk about the cases he was currently working. Trial lawyers are optimists. You have to be that way, to do the job successfully. But along with having that next legal victory out there on the horizon, they've also got their money out there someplace on a stick, a carrot on a stick that they never reach.

There has been many a trial lawyer who helped his clients, won big cases during the year, and looked forward to that year-end bonus, only to sit down with his accountant and find that the cash simply wasn't available to pay it.

This problem is made more acute by the habit these attorneys have of only reconciling their financial statements once a year. That means, come December, it's a full year's worth of ghost profits and case expenses that have passed through the firm, and taxes are coming due. Of course, one potential solution is to do financial statements more frequently, either monthly or quarterly, in order to know where your practice stands in terms of cash flow.

The use of a partner's cash to finance the practice is done as an afterthought. Most lawyers don't understand that the majority of other small-business owners, whether it's a manufacturer or a distributor or a service business, don't lend their own after-tax cash to their businesses interest-free. Usually, if the owners of a business put personal capital into the business, they will either create a note by which they're lending the money to the business and paying themselves back with interest, or, if they're putting additional capital in and there are multiple partners, they may obtain additional shares of stock as compensation for their capital contribution. This typically doesn't happen in a contingent-fee law practice because it's such a silent drain that the cash is going down. And because the books are typically only being reconciled once a year, they don't really realize that hey, I'm making profits, I'm winning cases, but it comes down to cash flow, the cash is flowing away from me instead of toward me.

Even if a contingent-fee law firm is going through a period of positive cash flow, the use of partners' cash to finance a law practice long-term should be considered in terms of the opportunity cost. As noted in the early part of this book, an opportunity cost is the cost of *not* taking a certain action. So in the case of using the partners' cash to fund case expense advances, the partners may think well, at least I don't have to borrow money and pay interest. And that's true. But because they've already earned those fees, paid their overhead, and paid their taxes, it's actually their personal after-tax cash that's tied up in the practice long-term. It's easy enough to acknowledge that it's not a good business decision to lend after-tax cash to anyone interest-free (as contingent-fee lawyers do to their firms). But it's also very relevant to consider the opportunity cost of not deploying that capital somewhere else, where it can yield a positive return.

So with opportunity costs, we're talking about the investment that wasn't made. Because opportunity costs are unseen, they're often not considered at all when making business decisions. But they are very real.

Imagine for a moment that you have $1 million of after-tax cash—your own money. Would you put it in a suitcase, lock it, and put it under your bed for 30 years? I think everybody would agree that it's not a good business decision to tie up capital like that. And yet that's exactly what most trial law practice partners do with regard to advancing case expenses. They're making a long-term, interest-free loan to their practice, and that's not a good business decision.

What is the opportunity cost for any individual law partner? Well, that depends upon the return they could be getting on that capital if they got it out and were able to do something with it. We find that the best investment most trial lawyers can make is in themselves – in their own practice, because they control that investment.

If you're a trial lawyer reading this, you know that if you could free up $100,000 of additional capital to spend in advertising this year, you could probably calculate pretty quickly what your return on

$100,000 would be. Is it 5 percent? Is it 10 percent? Is it 20 percent? The answer depends upon the individual practice, but it's certainly something north of zero!

Our monetary system in the United States favors growth in the money supply over time. Over the past 100 years that has consistently been the case, and lately even more so. The net effect of that over time is price inflation, and by extension the declining value of a dollar. Just as you used to be able to buy a loaf of bread for five cents, and now it costs three dollars, you could also think of that in reverse—the value of those five cents certainly went down. It was better to have used it when it had more buying power than to lock it away in some inaccessible place, such as case expenses.

During some of my presentations to lawyers on financial matters, I attempt to demonstrate this by taking out a $20 bill and offering it to one of the lawyers in the audience. He takes it willingly and says thank-you. Then I ask him a question—will he give me back the $20 if I promise to meet him one year later and give him $21? That's nominally an attractive offer, as it represents a five percent interest rate. The answer is always no, thank-you. At which point I up the year-later offer to $25. Again, the answer is always no. I'm now offering a 20 percent rate of return, but to no avail. The lawyer in the audience prefers to keep the $20 he has in hand.

My next offer is open-ended. It's actually a question: Is there some amount upwards of $25 that you'll take? If so, how high do I need to go? To put it another way, a bird in the hand is worth two in the bush!

Another way to think about the time value of money is to look at a simple chart. What is the value of cash invested at a certain percent over time? This chart approximates the declining purchasing power of $1,000,000 over 25 years, if invested at a zero rate of return, assuming a 3 percent annual monetary inflation rate.

Value of Cash Invested at 0%

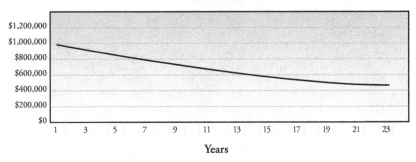

Years

Looking at a chart like this, and projecting into the future, it's hard to know exactly what the inflation rate will be, but it's going to be something. Therefore it's highly likely that the value of that dollar I've handed to the audience member will be a lot less 20 years from now. Meaning, its purchasing power will diminish. That $1,000,000 in after-tax cash that a partner has tied up in his practice, if they could get it out and spend it now, would provide much more purchasing power than if it were taken out 20 years from now when they wind their practice down. The value of that $1,000,000 is much greater now.

Now there are some advantages to the partners of a firm who use their own cash to fund their case expenses. First of all, they're not making interest payments to a lender. Also, there is no underwriting required. They're not applying for a loan anywhere, so it doesn't matter if they have a low credit rating. Nor will it matter if they have tax liens or if they lack tangible assets. They're not beholden to any lender. They're not at risk of foreclosure. It doesn't affect their credit score to loan money to their practice interest-free. So there are definitely advantages to the use of partner cash, especially compared to some of the options we've discussed in previous chapters.

CHAPTER THIRTEEN

Vendor Financing

V endor financing can take two forms. One would be unofficial or unapproved financing by the vendor, and the other would be negotiated (or explicit or approved) financing by the vendor. For the contingent-fee law firm, the vendors in question would be deposition services, court reporters, videographers, expert witnesses and the like.

Law firms will at times help finance some of their case expenses by delaying payments to vendors. Proceeding in this ad hoc manner is not recommended. It's probably in breach of an agreement, but in effect we've seen law firms that during a pinch have pushed all of their vendors' invoices back 30 days thereby effectively borrowing 30 days' worth of case expenses.

We have also seen savvy law firms negotiate with certain case-specific vendors to get better payment terms. They are able to get terms of net 60 instead of net 30, with no associated additional costs, and thus an interest-free loan for an extra 30 days. They enhance their profit-and-loss position just by aging their payables.

We have even seen some vendors willing to get paid on a delayed basis, agreeing to wait until a case is concluded. An example would be an expert witness that is willing to get paid out of the proceeds of the successful case. This is not particularly common, especially on the part of medical experts. They typically want an upfront retainer. But for certain other experts that are in highly competitive markets, we have definitely seen services provided on a contingent basis to the law firm. As a result, the firm is never out any cash for that particular vendor. The vendor provides the service and gets paid out of the proceeds of the case, which amounts to a simple pass-through.

It's difficult to pinpoint an average cost for vendor financing because it occurs on both an ad hoc and a negotiated basis. But if you assume that on the high end a vendor might charge an extra 10 percent per annum, and that on the low end it's zero percent especially for the contingent providers, you can come out with an average cost in the neighborhood of 5 percent.

Consider a deposition service that works regularly for a particular law firm. This service will handle multiple depositions per month and may bill on the order of $10,000 monthly. If the law firm is in a bit of a pinch, they may skip a month or two of payments, which obviously is difficult for the service provider because their regular stream of monthly income from that law firm gets put off for a month or two. They have to find capital somewhere to fill that gap until the law firm can get current on its payments. The firm is transferring its capital problem to its vendor.

Using vendors as a bank in this manner is not officially recognized in the marketplace. It can cause great tension between a law firm and its vendors I make note of it simply because it's one of the forms of financing that occurs. Many times it is impromptu, and done because the law firm simply doesn't have the cash to make payments. Other times, though, it is negotiated upfront between the law firm and its vendor.

Whether or not a vendor is willing to extend terms to a law firm is largely dependent on how much competition that vendor faces and how much volume it does with the firm requesting the ad hoc loan. If the law firm is their biggest customer, or one of their biggest the firm will have a lot more leverage with which to negotiate. Another factor will be the vendor's own liquidity or access to additional capital to deal with the fluctuating cash flow from its clients.

Many service providers to law firms are small mom-and-pop operations. They are unlikely to feel they have much leverage with the law firm. Conversely, many of the medical doctors who do expert witness work in medical malpractice cases might require a check upfront for $10,000 just to review a file. So the more cachet that a vendor has, and the less competition they face, obviously the more leverage they will have to be able to demand terms that are favorable to them.

Vendor financing in the non-negotiated form is really a form of defaulting on an agreement. It is not a practice that's good for the law firm, not to mention, for the vendor. However, when this is negotiated upfront, it can be very effective. If a law firm can sit down with its top three or four case expense vendors and negotiate better payment terms with them, that is definitely a way of enhancing liquidity, and it can potentially be done at a fairly low cost.

When we underwrite, we look at the balance sheets of law firms, occasionally noting that they have a large accounts-payable balance. When we query it, they will say that they have negotiated terms with some of their vendors, and thus have a large open balance. And that open balance represents a form of financing. Vendors to law firms often pre-print invoices noting their intention to assess 1.5 percent per month for late bills. Most of them don't enforce that. If they can just get the bill paid, they'll be happy to waive the late fee. Annualized, that 1.5 percent comes to an 18 percent interest rate. If a vendor is going to negotiate upfront, they may want something in return. They may give you net 120 terms, but the price they set for the service provided might be 10 percent higher.

Pre-negotiated vendor financing of case expenses does have several benefits. There are no credit checks and usually no security interest is granted and no UCCs or liens are filed on the firm's assets. There is no underwriting process for vendor financing and it is cash flow-positive, especially if the vendor agrees to wait to get paid out of the proceeds of the case.

A few general negatives are that the vendor may tend to give priority to its other law firm customers if they know they will get paid promptly by them, thereby potentially reducing the service level being provided to the firm being financed. Also, vendor financing may not be dependable, because the vendor could decide to halt the practice more or less at will.

CHAPTER FOURTEEN

Bank Lines of Credit

O utside of partners' cash, the bank line of credit is surely the second-most common method law firms use to fund case expenses. Typically the law firm is setting up a plain-vanilla, one-size-fits-all credit line. You are actually not compelled to do a lot of shopping between banks, as there is so much consistency in what's offered. Typical bank business lines of credit are homogenous in terms of pricing and underwriting because of the highly competitive market and the fact that banks all have roughly the same borrowing costs and regulatory constraints. Interestingly, even if a particular bank was able to negotiate a higher-than-average interest rate with the borrower, most of their credit departments would balk at doing the loan. Generally, they consider anything over about prime plus two to be a high-risk loan. Because there's so much competition in the marketplace among banks, their credit departments normally figure that if someone is willing to pay prime plus three or four percent there must be something wrong with the loan from a credit perspective.

The result is that most banks have very similar pricing—an effective rate that will be somewhere in the prime minus one to prime plus one range. This points out an obvious advantage in choosing a bank credit line for your case financing—you will not pay a particularly high interest rate. (At this writing, the Prime Rate stood at 3.25 percent.)

Likewise, the terms are usually easy to understand and the loan documents and the structure are very main stream, as well.

There are a couple of potential negatives when using bank lines of credit. One of the negatives is that the credit function in banks can be cyclical when it comes to what you might call marginal industries. Depending upon market conditions, bank ownership changes and management changes, they can in short order make wholesale changes to the types of business they want to be in.

An example of this occurred recently in my hometown of Cleveland, Ohio. A large bank from out of state bought a Cleveland-based bank. One of the changes they made coming into the Cleveland market was to summarily decide that printers were a poor risk. If you were a printer and you had been a line of credit customer with the bank being acquired, the new bank invited you to go elsewhere.

This is the kind of thing that can happen to any industry, but it most often happens even at the fringes of certain industries. Often the dynamic for loan applicants to banks is this: The shorter the story, the more likely you are to get approved. So if you're in a very well-understood, stable, long-term industry, it's much easier to get approved (and renewed later).

If you manufacture a common household item there's a strong market, and the product isn't seasonal, it's a lot easier to get approved than if you're a contingent-fee law practice. That's simply because banks can understand the manufacturer and its business. They make a tangible product. They store it in a warehouse, ship it, bill for it, then collect for it. That's a business model banks don't have trouble comprehending.

However, with a contingent-fee law practice, they first will come in and say well, let us see your list of accounts receivable. And there really won't be any accounts receivable as far as the banker is concerned because the contingent-fee law practice has not billed anyone for any services. Revenues are not due to them until each case is successfully resolved. This throws the bank credit manager a curveball.

They also like to see assets backing a line of credit, and of course, with law practices, the balance sheets are typically very thin, showing very little in the way of physical assets. Nor is there often much in the way of cash assets to lend against. When law practices come into cash—when they build up positive net worth through surplus income—it doesn't stay in their account, it typically goes out to pay for overhead and case expense. If there is any excess cash flow after that, it normally goes out as compensation to the partners of the firm.

To be fair to the credit departments at banks, it is their job to think though the worst-case scenarios in order to protect the bank's assets, the investment of the bank's shareholders and the security of their depositors' funds. When they make a real estate loan and it goes bad, they know how to foreclose on the property and sell it to get made whole. In the case of a manufacturer, they can foreclose on the accounts receivable and/or inventory of the borrower and liquidate that, once again getting made whole. But when they think about a contingent-fee law firm loan going bad, they are not really sure how they would pursue their collateral, if it is just the cases of the law firm. So many times they will seek other collateral for the line of credit, such as the personal assets of the partners, other real estate, and the like.

Because of the hesitancy a bank can harbor toward this business model, their approvals of credit lines are subject to a certain fickleness. The bank approves you one year, but they may come back next year and decide not to renew. They may contact the firm midstream and say we'd like you to find another bank.

Banks in general won't be able to underwrite as large a line as a non-bank finance company will. One of the challenges banks face is that they're very heavily regulated by either their state or by federal regulating agencies. They have very strict capitalization requirements, underwriting requirements and documentation requirements. That in itself can make it difficult for a bank to be flexible regarding terms or documentation.

Over the years, we have noticed that, generally, local banks tend to be more flexible in lending to contingent-fee law firms. They seem to be more willing to work with these firms. I attribute this to their flatter organizational structure—it's a shorter distance between the bank president and the loan officer. They are able to be more adaptable to varying business models and can take the time to understand contingent-fee practices.

There is one other negative with bank lines of credit. It comes into play when the bank activates its requirement for the borrower, the law firm, to pay the line of credit down to a zero balance once a year for up to 30 days. This requirement is often put into commercial lines of credit by banks because a bank doesn't really want to be in a long-term "evergreen" arrangement with its borrowers. Banks typically view working capital lines of credit as seasonal.

Banks understand a seasonal business model, in which a company may need to ramp up its inventory or hiring based on the seasonal nature of its business. And they look for that borrower to be able to pay that line back down when the slow season has passed. Obviously law firms are not seasonal, and this requirement does not work well for law firms. Part of the requirement to zero out the balance once a year is that fickleness quotient. The banks want to know that they can decide not to renew you. If they require you to pay down to zero 30 days out of every year, that gives them the ability, when they get to zero, to simply not renew you and be out of the relationship if they wish to.

To some extent I agree with the banks' reasoning on some of this. Not so much the seasonal aspect of it, but the fact that it's not healthy for a business to have indefinite debt and be continually eating the interest expenses. It's not a good business model to be financing short-term benefits with long-term borrowing.

Beware of Flat Fees

Banks love to emphasize a low interest rate and then make up their profits in fees. Example: A line of credit for $500,000 with a 2 percent annual fee and an annual interest rate of 5 percent could really have a much higher effective rate if the line is not fully used. Assuming an average balance of $250,000 during the year, annual interest payments would be $12,500 (5 percent x $250,000). But when you add in the annual fee of $10,000 (2 percent x $500,000) the actual effective interest rate is not 5 percent...but 9 percent!

$$(\$12,500 + 10,000)/\$250,000 =$$
$$9 \text{ percent}$$

So watch those fees and consider their likely impact on your overall costs when comparing loans or making a decision to borrow.

CHAPTER FIFTEEN

Loan with Interest Pass-Through

We have looked at many of the unique challenges that contingent-fee law firms face regarding access to capital. There is, however, one unique opportunity that many firms don't realize is available to them: A loan with interest pass-through. "Interest pass-through" is a term used to describe the passing of borrowing costs from a third party lender through the law firm to the actual cases. In contingent-fee cases, the normal procedure is for any third-party costs to be paid from the case, including such expenses as expert witnesses, charts for the courtroom, deposition fees, travel expenses, etc. What many firms don't realize is that borrowing costs, if properly accounted for and disclosed up front to the client, can also qualify as case-specific expenses that can be passed through just like other items.

The state supreme courts and ethics panels around the country have consistently ruled that law firms owe their clients the best possible legal representation, but they do not owe the client an interest-free loan, which is what case expenses advanced by the law firm represent (see IRS Private Letter Ruling 8246013, 6/30/1982, IRC Sec(s). 162). So there is no moral, ethical or legal requirement for a law firm to advance the case expenses out of the law firm's after-tax cash, in effect making an interest-free loan to its client during the case. Although that has become the tradition, it's not a requirement.

What that translates into is an opportunity. If a law firm is able to borrow on a case-specific basis and have all its borrowing costs tracked on a case-specific basis, it is able to get reimbursed from the case settlement or judgment for not only the expert witness fees and other charges, but also for the borrowing costs.

No law firm wins every case, so therefore, on the cases that are not won; the borrowing cost and other witness fees, etc. are not reimbursed to the law firm. But a loan with interest pass-through can be one of the lowest-cost methods of access to capital for a law firm.

Based on the most recent Department of Justice statistics available (NCJ-153177, NCJ-179769), approximately 97 percent of all civil disputes in the United States conclude without going to trial. Given that it would be illogical for the plaintiff to settle out of court for less than their expenses and some kind of fee, you can deduce that 97 percent of the time law firms are recouping their case expenses from their cases. Therefore, on a loan with interest pass-through, you can assume that, on average, 97 percent of the time the law firm will be able to get reimbursed for its borrowing costs thereby passing through 97 percent of the cost of the borrowing to its cases. The net result is a very, very low cost of funds. It is difficult to pinpoint due to the varying terms from lenders and the variable win rate at law firms, but I believe a good estimate is between 0.5 and 0.8 percent. That would be the net annual cost of funds to the law firm for borrowing against its advanced case expenses.

In an area fraught with disadvantages, this is an advantage. Contingent-fee law firms can exploit it to offset some of the limitations and difficulties they face in trying to access capital in the marketplace. If a firm is able to leverage the partners' after-tax cash that would otherwise be tied up in case expenses—and if it can do so at a net annual cost of well under 1 percent—it seems quite obvious that those funds could easily be deployed elsewhere to great advantage.

Now there are some caveats to this concept. The law firm should explain up front and in writing (in the attorney-client agreement) that it will be borrowing for the case expenses and that the borrowing costs will be passed through to the case.

There needs to be a careful distinction made between charging the client interest vs. passing through interest from a third-party lender. In most states (but not all), a law firm is precluded from lending money directly to a client and charging them interest. If a law firm does lend money to a client, this act could conceivably categorize it as a consumer lender and make it subject to a host of state and federal regulations, licensing requirements and reporting protocols. Further, it seems that interest charged to a client would qualify as taxable income and should probably be reported as such for tax purposes.

However, passing through interest from a third party avoids all of those pitfalls, provided that the borrowing costs are carefully calculated and accounted for to the penny so as to ensure that the client's case is only being charged for interest costs associated with his or her case (see Chittenden v. State Farm 00-C-0414, Louisiana Supreme Court).

So there is a technical challenge here and there are a limited number of lenders in the marketplace that have the software and sophistication to be able to track a law firm's line of credit on a case-by-case basis. After all, most firms have hundreds of cases, and some have thousands. Also, presently these lenders seem to be very selective regarding credit approval for lines of credit. Sometimes even tighter than banks! But if a firm can qualify for one of these programs, they will have access to capital that is well below the cost of even a bank line. These types of lines of credit also typically require a relatively high degree of reporting and documentation to be provided by the law firms.

Important: It is necessary to understand and abide by all ethics and legal guidelines that exist in your state. This book is not intended to dispense legal advice. Do your homework before proceeding with a loan with interest pass-through to make sure you are proceeding in a manner consistent with all applicable laws and guidelines.

Summary:

Here is a graphical summary of the ten sources of capital available to contingent-fee law firms discussed in the preceding chapters. The effective annual interest rates are based upon publicly available information. These rates do not include potential non-economic benefits of some sources of capital such as risk abatement, access to other law firms' expertise, etc.

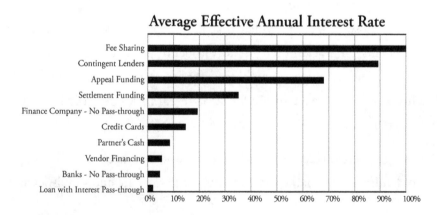

PART 3
Application

CHAPTER SIXTEEN

About That Loan...

Too often, the sales literature and websites for lending companies that serve contingent-fee law firms are vague and confusing. Whether that is intentional or not, I cannot say. But I do know that some of the sales reps in the industry have used this vagueness to their advantage by selectively communicating the details of their product offering. They tend to be non-specific and in fact take advantage of the lack of financial savvy and training of the lawyers they presume to serve. Often their presentations are based on what the lawyer wants to hear, not on the reality of the product they have to offer.

Many of these lenders' promotional materials do not state their fees, rates and terms in writing. They intentionally avoid that. They will discuss rates on the telephone, that's true. But even after a loan application is opened and being discussed, the law firm may not see the actual interest rate until they get the final loan documents. At that point, they are very likely surprised to see numbers they weren't expecting (if in fact they bothered to read the loan documents) or unexpected fees that had not been discussed to that point.

The vast majority of lenders do not give written term sheets because if they were to disclose everything upfront, the law firm would very likely turn away. They'd rather spend a month or two or three underwriting and get the law firm heavily involved in the process. I believe that they foresee a higher chance of closing a deal that way. Their hope (and it's often fulfilled) is that no one at the firm actually reads the contracts!

When I refer to undisclosed rates and terms in these offers, I'm talking about basic information your average consumer buying a home would be provided. Information is withheld with impunity because lending to law firms is typically considered a commercial transaction (in other words, not a consumer lending product). The vast majority of states regulate commercial lending transactions very lightly, if at all. By now we're accustomed to the various consumer protections in a lender-borrower transaction—we benefit from them whenever we borrow money to buy a car or buy a house. Those commonplace protections are not available to most trial law firms, again because loans to law firms are categorized as commercial, not consumer oriented.

Real-life Story

I recently consulted with an attorney who had taken out a loan with one of these lenders. He had failed to look at the paperwork carefully, signed the agreement and turned it over to his bookkeeper to manage the program, so to speak. He didn't even realize that he was paying 20 percent interest per year! His loan amount was half a million dollars, which meant his debt services was about $100,000 per year. Now, seven years along, he has been paying $100,000 in interest annually—money he could have been using all along to help more clients and to get better results for them. Once he realized how much he was spending on interest every year, he of course wanted to exit the situation immediately, but was hard-pressed to find additional, alternative forms of capital, because he had borrowed so much on that one loan. Relief from this payment burden could hardly be obtained in short order. It would take several years and several hundred thousand more in payments before he could work his way out of the relationship.

All that being said, here are a few recommendations if you are applying for a new loan or line of credit, or negotiating a renewal.

Get a Term Sheet – Be sure to get a detailed term sheet from the lender. Do not rely upon the verbal commitment of the bank or loan company's representative regarding the important details of the loan. The term sheet should be on the lender's letterhead, should be signed by an officer of the lender and at a minimum should clearly state :

- The interest rate and whether it will be simple interest or compounded.

- Deferred interest, if any.

- All fees:
  - Application fees
  - Origination fees
  - Annual fees
  - Documentation fees
  - Legal fees
  - Renewal fees

- A detailed collateral description.

- Pre-payment penalty (if any.)

- Restrictions on the size or timing of funding requests (if any.)

If the term sheet does not mention one or more of the above items, ask about each of them and have them confirm their answers in writing.

Watch Those Fees! – Lenders love to emphasize a low interest rate and then make up their profits in fees. Example: A line of credit for $500,000 with a 2 percent annual fee and an annual interest rate of 5 percent could really have a much higher effect rate if the line is not fully used. Assuming an average balance of $250,000 during the year, annual interest payments would be $12,500 (5 percent x $250,000). But when you add in the annual fee of $10,000 (2 percent x $500,000) the actual effective interest rate is not 5 percent...but 9 percent! (($12,500 + 10,000)/$250,000)= 9 percent). So watch those fees and consider their likely impact on your overall costs when comparing loans or making a decision to borrow.

Check References – This is less important with a bank line of credit, but if you are considering a loan from a non-bank finance company, you should absolutely get three references from them that you can call and ask questions such as: How long have you had a loan with this lender? Have the rates and fees been what you expected? Have there ever been delays in processing your funding requests? Are you happy with their service? Have there been any hidden fees? Would you do business with them again?

Ask About Funding Sources – As above, this applies mainly to non-bank lenders. Many law firm borrowers were left high and dry during the 2008-2010 credit crunch when the majority of non-bank lenders found their own funding sources drying up. Many lenders in the market had to freeze their existing borrowers out of new fundings and some had to call in their lines because their funding sources (private equity, equity funds, hedge funds) demanded it. Look for a lender with a solid track record that is not dependent upon volatile funding sources. This can also be discovered when checking references.

Check Out Your Bank – Banks are required to submit financial data to their regulators on a quarterly basis. This information is available to the public free of charge at http://www.fdic.gov/bankfind. You might not understand everything you see there, but it's informative to see if your bank is operating at a profit or not! You can also see whether they are growing vs. shrinking assets, incurring large losses, etc. If they appear to be having trouble, you may find them being swallowed up by another bank soon.

Hire the Right Attorney – Most contingent-fee lawyers are not well versed in contract law and yet so often they try to be their own lawyer when they go out to source capital. Spending a few hundred dollars on a trusted contract lawyer who will review the documents before the transaction is always prudent. That being said, understand that the attorney will be looking to totally pick apart the agreement and tell you all the things that are potentially wrong with it. You can use their feedback to negotiate the best possible business deal and you will be better informed about the potential pitfalls of the relationship.

Do read the contracts – It's amazing how many lawyers do not even read their own loan documents before they sign them. They sign them and move on. You should always read the documents before signing them. But do bear in mind that many lenders take their loans and pool them or securitize them together into the market-place. And the lender's funding source(s) may place limitations on the number of contract changes they are permitted to enter. Because of that, most lenders are not able to make significant changes to their loan documents, but at least know what it says so you know what you're getting into and perhaps you can get them to agree to amend one or two provisions to the agreement.

Be Careful – Lastly, be very careful when borrowing funds for your law firm. Too many excellent lawyers find themselves in trouble because they borrow too much money, borrow at very high interest rates or borrow long-term to fund-short term projects. The best borrowing (if you do any) is tied to specific cases so that discipline is imposed to pay down the loan principal as cases conclude. Borrowing in this manner can also enable the firm to pass the borrowing costs through to the cases, if tracked properly by the lender. Debt can be a useful tool for a law firm, but it can also be a dangerous trap if not implemented properly.

Beware of Trade Association Endorsements and Preferred Vendor Programs!

Most trade associations (including those for trial lawyers) have programs that provide endorsements or lists of preferred vendors on their websites and in their publications. These programs can include all sorts of potential law firm vendors, not just financial services providers. The fact is, however, that these "endorsements" or preferred-vendor programs are primarily a means of raising money for the associations. Most of the time, the "endorsement" simply goes to the highest bidder, who may or may not have the best products and services for the membership of the association. So you need to beware of such endorsements and do your own research when considering vendors. *Do not* assume that the association has carefully researched alternatives and selected the best possible vendors. As always, buyer beware!

CHAPTER SEVENTEEN

Onward

The best avenue for accessing capital can vary considerably from firm to firm. Primary factors affecting the choice include: overall net worth of the law firm and its partners, how long the firm has been in practice; the credit scores of its partners; and the amount of revenue being generated in relation to borrowing needs. Other considerations include how much time the firm has to complete applications and provide documentation, and how open the firm is to laying off risk from the law firm to a contingent lender of some sort (whether through a commercial company doing contingent lending or another law firm that would do fee-sharing).

These are just some of the factors that should weigh into the decision-making process. Examining these questions, one can place a firm somewhere on a spectrum from low to higher risk. The more a firm is operated "on the fly," in our experience, the higher its capital costs are going to be. Conversely, the firms that are the best run, that have partners with the highest credit scores, with the best net worth, the longest and best track record in their practice, are going to be able to access capital much less expensively than competitors are.

Although the skill of a law firm's lawyers and the quality of its cases are important components for success, a firm that has adequate access to favorably priced capital has a significant advantage. When you are able to access capital in larger amounts and at lower cost than your competitors, you end up hiring the best experts. You produce better advertising and more people see that advertising. You have a larger and more skilled staff. Your clients get better attention. Your offices make a better impression. Now, if you can add those personal qualities of legal knowledge, integrity and diligence—all together that is a formidable package.

Probably the most important outcome of a best-practices approach to finance management is that lawyers can leverage themselves that much more. They can grow their practices and help that many more clients. A law firm's client is not helped when they have a highly skilled lawyer who's not properly capitalized or not properly managed financially. It doesn't matter how good a lawyer you are if you don't have the cash to pay for that expert witness at trial.

You need both sides of the coin. You need excellent legal skills and you need excellent business execution to truly benefit the client. If I ever have to hire a personal injury lawyer, by all means I'm going to see if they're the best possible lawyer I can find, but the other step I take will be to ask to see proof of their financial capabilities. I'll want assurances as to their ability to take on my case successfully, along with all the other cases they have, and not have to skimp on important case development costs like expert witnesses and deposition costs. That would absolutely be part of the selection process for me. I will want to see their financials, and hear what their plan is for accessing capital over the next two years while they're taking my case. On a less obvious but equally important level, I'm looking at their ability to focus due to freedom from unnecessary stress. When you're head hits the pillow at night, are you thinking about not having the capital to pursue your cases?

That's a frustrating position to be in. It's caused a lot of lawyers to make bad decisions. The clients and cases are in front of them, the only missing element is cash, so they decide to take on a very expensive loan. Or they fill out applications for more credit cards. What may end up happening is that they get frustrated because they can't get the results they want for their clients, due to the reality that they lack the liquidity to bring the cases to full development. In that case they may decide to either not take certain cases, or turn certain cases over to other law firms and forego large amounts of fee income. The stress level in practices that are managed on the fly or by the seat of the pants when it comes to business issues and capitalization is much higher.

In the opposite scenario, with skillfully managed finances, confidence in the workings of the operation and freedom from distraction extends throughout the law firm. Picture a firm with four partners and seven associates, all of them working on cases or evaluating possible cases. They meet on Mondays. They get their marching orders. They know, each and every one, that their activities are funded. The firm is liquid. Everyone knows that the firm has its capital source at a very affordable rate. All things being equal, that law firm must be a good place to work.

If that describes your law firm, it's not a matter that you stumbled into it. Or that you achieved this stability in the normal course of running your practice. The minds of most successful contingent-fee attorneys aren't naturally inclined toward income statements and balance sheets. In my experience, they tend to focus on the legal issues, the client's predicament and the adversarial process of working against big corporations and insurance companies that want to avoid doing what's right. Contingent-fee attorneys seldom relish Excel spreadsheets and interest-rate comparisons. It's just not in the DNA.

I tell attorneys I work with, you're going to deal with these financial issues now or you will deal with them later. You can make a decision to pay up front—devote some of your time and resources to properly think through these issues, plan them, and execute a good capital structure plan. You could also choose to pay on the back end, in which case you will spend at least as much time trying to fix problems later.

Minimize Net Interest Costs

As a general rule, you should strive to minimize the amount of interest you pay each year by borrowing in a very strategic, controlled way. Here's a good exercise: At the end of each year (or right now!) total up the interest that appears on your income statement from loans at your firm, along with any interest from credit cards that your firm may have. Subtract the interest that you recoup from your cases (if any) and take a look at that number. Ask yourself: What did I get for that money? If you're not sure...there's a problem! Too many firms borrow money for short term needs (advertising, bonuses, etc.) but then never pay it back during the good times. The result is effectively a permanent debt that does nothing but steal profits out of the partners' pockets without giving back much in the way of tangible benefits. If your firm is going to borrow money, especially for case expenses, consider recouping the interest from your cases. It's legal, it's ethical and there are lenders in the marketplace that can track the interest for you on a case-by-case basis to make it easy on your staff.

Don't Wait Until You Need Capital to Secure It

Many law firms wait until they have their worst year ever, and are stuck in a cash-flow crunch before trying to access capital through a loan of some type. Even if they can secure a loan under those conditions, it's going to be very expensive. Access capital from a position of strength. Don't wait until your credit score goes down, or you need the money, or you're having a soft revenue year. The old adage that banks don't lend money to people who need it is true. In fact, any smart lender would not do business with a law firm that really *needed* money. The key is to establish capital relationships during your *best* years, not your worst.

Create a Rainy Day Fund

Available borrowing capacity on credit cards is NOT a rainy day fund! Many, many law firms and their partners are maintaining six-figure credit card debt over 10 or 15 cards because they have used them as a "rainy day" fund. Obviously it's extremely expensive to do that and it just digs a deep hole that is difficult to ever escape. Many others simply have multiple credit cards with open balances available in case of unforeseen need. But I'll say it again...a credit card is not an emergency fund. An emergency fund is cash in the bank. A credit card is the pathway to easy but expensive future debt. It is a prudent move personally and professionally to put aside some cash so that you can deal with the unforeseen without having to dig a deep, expensive hole.

Pay Down the Most Expensive Debt First

As we process applications from law firms, it is not at all unusual to see a firm or partner that has $20,000 of cash in the bank and at the same time is carrying a $20,000 balance on multiple credit cards. Obviously in a situation like that there is an opportunity to eliminate a lot of interest expense by simply paying off some credit cards rather have them sit out there with $20,000 on them for another year at 18 percent (or even higher). If you have excess cash at the end of the month, review any outstanding debt you have and consider paying some of it down.

Know Your Credit Score

Do you know what your credit score is? You should! Set a tickler in your calendar to remind yourself to check your credit score at least once a year. Free services like www.freecreditreport.com are available to make it quick, easy and free. You don't want to wait until it's time to apply for a loan or a lease to do this. You may find that your score has dropped due to an error at a reporting agency or by your bookkeeper. That lower score could result in costly delays or higher rates of interest paid. It could even result in your application being rejected since many banks have been steadily raising their minimum credit-score requirements over the past few years.

Monitor Liens

Do you know what liens are filed on your firm and on you personally? You may be surprised at what is in place. We have a client in California that recently came up for its annual renewal of our agreement. As part of the renewal we did our standard check to make sure nobody else had filed UCCs on the firm's accounts receivable. That routine check turned up a $2 million lien against the law firm! It was filed by a disgruntled former client of the firm.

This individual had logged on to the California Secretary of State's website and created a fictitious UCC filing against the law firm for $2 million. The firm didn't know it was there until we checked and let them know about it. I'm not sure they would have known until they had to go find some other financing and it could have potentially blown a deal for them. Because the firm had never granted a security interest to the filer of the UCC, the UCC was worthless, but it still raised a red flag during the renewal process and could have delayed any new transactions that the law firm had been seeking.

So it's important to monitor liens filed on you and your law firm. It only takes a few moments to check UCC filings using LexisNexis® or Westlaw®. This is another good annual exercise. Even if you see the UCCs filed that you expect, such as from your current lenders, look closely at the description of collateral in the filings. It is very common for a borrower to think their line of credit is secured by their real estate but for the lender to actually file on the firm's accounts receivable or even all the assets of the firm. Again, this can cause costly delays when applying for or renewing loans or leases and it costs nothing to monitor.

Monitor and Build Your Net Worth

My experience has been that the partners of contingent-fee law firms consistently overestimate the market value of their law firm. They are often content having all of their net worth tied up in their law firm. But the reality is that a typical contingent-fee law firm has very little equity value in and of itself. The balance sheet typically shows little in the way of assets. So the net value of a law firm – (also referred to as book value), which is the difference between the assets and the liabilities—is extremely low. Often the book value is zero, or even a negative number.

Of course it's natural for the partners in the firm to think they have a very valuable entity. It is valuable to them because it generates cash flow and incomes, and provides a living for its employees and its partners. However, most contingent-fee lawyers fail to understand that a lender looking at a law firm is not putting stock in future earnings. When a potential lender looks at a law firm, it wants to see collateral. The banker wants to be able to conceive of a plan to get repaid in case things go wrong. When evaluating the potential loan, the lender wants to know that they will be able to use the collateral to get paid. If the collateral is real estate or an automobile, a lender can simply foreclose on it, sell it in the marketplace, and pocket the proceeds which are hopefully enough to cover the loan balance.

But in the case of a contingent-fee law firm, can a bank step in and keep the cases? What are they going to do with them? They have no answer for that. A bank doesn't want the cases and a bank can't own a law firm.

Now of course a law firm is extremely valuable to the partners. But that does not mean it has a lot of market value because the market value of anything is the price at which the asset would trade in a competitive auction environment. Realistically, what would a contingent-fee law firm sell for in an auction environment? It's a fairly illiquid asset in large part because the partners are typically part of the brand. So if it's Kyle Jeffries LLC, Kyle Jeffries is the brand. Can Kyle Jeffries sell Kyle Jeffries LLC to someone other than Kyle Jeffries? Of what value would it be, even to some other lawyer? Kyle Jeffries might be able to sell his cases to another lawyer, or transfer them, but again, the value of the cases is very subjective and is open to interpretation on a case-by-case basis.

Therefore... build net worth that goes *beyond* your law firm. Get professional investment advice and then put in place a system of saving money and investing in assets in *addition* to your firm (but not assets that take your time away from your firm like other businesses). You want to accumulate liquid, tangible net worth that can be easily valued in the marketplace. Later in life you'll be glad you did. And your access to future capital will be greatly enhanced.

One last note on net worth: Visit www.Zillow.com or other market-based real estate valuation websites at least once a year to see what your real estate is really worth. Unfortunately for many of us, it is not as valuable as it used to be!

Review Your Bank Statements

It is important for the partners of a law firm to personally review their trust account and operating account bank statements each month. Ideally the statements should be mailed to the managing partner and be opened by the partner, not a member of the staff. The partner should then examine the statements for anything that looks out of place and should spot check a portion of the payments flowing out of the account for proper documentation. It should be made known amongst the staff that the statements are being carefully reviewed and will be questioned from time to time as a preventive measure against potential fraud. Also, if the firm has access to any lines of credit or has its own credit card, those monthly statements should also be personally reviewed by the managing partner. This is a critical issue. Over the years, we have seen several instances of fraud at firms involving seasoned, trusted personal friends employed by the firm. I am talking about personal friends of the partners, people they might have gone to church with, embezzling money over time to the tune of hundreds of thousands of dollars—over a million dollars, in a few of the cases we've seen.

If you have adequate staffing, put checks and balances in place so that the same people who are writing the checks for the firm are not the ones signing them. Also, put in place a system where whoever is writing the checks for the firm is not the person who opens the bank statement and reconciles the account at the end of the month.

Sadly, it is often the person on your team that you trust the most that ends up surprising you with fraudulent activity. Better to create a situation whereby it is as difficult as possible for someone to perpetrate such acts. Everyone wins when frauds is prevented.

Pay Attention to Your Financial Statements

Like the owners of any business, the partners of contingent-fee law firms divide time between financial activities (reviewing statements, managing cash, etc.) and non-financial activities (taking care of clients, marketing, hiring, training, etc.). My experience has been that, compared to most business people, trial lawyers generally spend far too little time reviewing and understanding the key financial reports at their firm. This is understandable, because contrary to popular opinion, the trial lawyers I know did not get into the practice of law primarily as a means of making money. They do what they do because they enjoy helping people. So the financial aspect of law practice may not really appeal to them. They'd rather be taking care of a client or working on a case. More often than not, they may only look at their financial statements once a year, and even then it is done briefly and without a lot of understanding. After all, they don't teach financial accounting in law school! And while the firm's bookkeeper may do a great job with day-to-day matters, they are rarely equipped to analyze the practice and advise the partners on financial matters.

The problem that I often see developing from this situation is that if the financial end of the practice is not adequately managed, small problems become big ones and ultimately the practice is not able to maximize its ability to serve its clients, regardless of the good intentions of the partners. So I recommend a few simple steps that I believe will pay back the relatively small cost in time and expenses many times over.

First, if you don't have a person in house who is capable of preparing financial statements, contract it out to a competent CPA. The statements should include an Income Statement, Balance Sheet and Cash Flow Statement. They should be reviewed at least quarterly, but monthly is ideal, especially if it is a medium to large law firm.

Secondly, pay your CPA to take the initiative to schedule the regular meeting at which you will review the statements together. Also, pay this CPA to critique what they see. What looks out of place to them? How would an outsider (e.g., a bank) view these statements? What expenses look too high? Where is most of the cash in the firm going? That's the discussion you need to be having.

I guarantee this will be painful at first but you will learn a lot about your practice and will be able to spot small problems before they become large. You'll see exactly where your strengths and weaknesses are financially and will be better equipped in the long term to seek justice on behalf your clients more effectively. You'll also be able to worry less and concentrate on your cases better knowing that you have put in place a disciplined system of regular financial review. And should you ever decide to seek outside capital, your chances of success will be much greater and with lower costs.

Conclusion

If you are a trial lawyer, I hope you have found this book to be useful in your practice. If you pick up even one useful idea, my mission will have been accomplished. I believe in what you do and this book is an attempt, mainly, to help as many trial lawyers as possible as they continue their daily battle against the Goliaths out there.

If you are not a trial lawyer, I hope you too will have found this book to be useful in reaching a more accurate understanding of what trial lawyers do and the considerable challenges they face.

I hope you never have to hire a personal injury lawyer…but if you do, you should hope they have read this book!

Index

A

abatement, 11, 53, 56, 59, 64, 68, 69, 72, 110

accounts, 34, 35, 36, 40, 43, 64, 78, 80, 86, 88, 99, 103, 124, 125

ACI, 17

appeal, 67, 68, 69, 128

assets, 24, 28, 29, 33, 34, 36, 38, 40, 44, 57, 71, 72, 73, 77, 78, 80, 86, 95, 100, 103, 104, 117, 125, 127

association, 118

attorney-client, 37, 69, 109

B

bankfind, 117

bankrupt, 72

banks, 28, 37, 38, 45, 77, 78, 79, 86, 101, 102, 103, 104, 105, 110, 123, 124

best-practices, 120

bonuses, 74, 122

borrowing, 33, 40, 64, 72, 81, 82, 97, 101, 105, 107, 108, 109, 118, 119, 122, 123

budget, 82

C

California, 21, 124, 125

capital
  capital-sourcing, 11
  undercapitalized, 41
  well-capitalized, 77
case-expense, 58, 75
cash-flow, 123
  neutral, 57, 72
  positive, 29, 44, 56, 57, 61, 86, 92, 93, 100, 103
caveats, 109
cephalgia, 22
champerty, 40
collateral, 28, 33, 34, 35, 36, 46, 47, 56, 57, 64, 71, 78, 80, 86, 103, 115, 125, 126
consumable, 81
contingency, 32, 79
  contingent-fee, 11, 17, 33, 34, 35, 36, 37, 38, 39, 40, 41, 43, 45, 51, 52, 77, 78, 80, 82, 85, 89, 90, 91, 92, 93, 102, 103, 104, 107, 110, 113, 117, 121, 125, 126, 128
contractors, 80
contractual, 37
corporations, 15, 16, 17, 24, 40, 122
costs, 16, 23, 37, 45, 46, 51, 68, 93, 94, 97, 101, 105, 107, 108, 109, 116, 118, 119, 120, 125, 130
CPA, 52, 129
credit, 27, 33, 47, 56, 57, 60, 64, 65, 68, 72, 75, 78, 83, 85, 86, 87, 88, 95, 100, 101, 102, 103, 104, 105, 110, 115, 116, 119, 121, 122, 123, 124, 125, 127
  credit-score, 124

customer, 81, 86, 99, 102

D

debt, 47, 82, 85, 88, 105, 114, 122, 123, 124
decision-making, 74, 119
deposition, 37, 97, 98, 107, 120
development, 39, 120, 121
doctor, 22
documentation, 73, 104, 110, 119, 127

E

embezzling, 128
endorsement, 118
equity, 31, 36, 44, 77, 80, 117, 125
estate, 36, 103, 104, 125, 126, 127
ethics, 107, 110
expenses, 24, 27, 28, 32, 33, 35, 36, 37, 38, 39, 40, 41, 43, 44, 46, 47, 56, 57, 58, 59, 61, 71, 89, 90, 91, 92, 93, 94, 95, 97, 100, 101, 105, 107, 108, 109, 122, 129

F

fees, 30, 35, 36, 37, 38, 39, 43, 44, 47, 56, 57, 58, 61, 63, 64, 65, 67, 68, 71, 73, 80, 81, 82, 91, 93, 105, 107, 108, 113, 115, 116
fee-sharing, 56, 57, 59, 60, 61, 119
finance, 28, 51, 56, 65, 67, 68, 77, 78, 79, 80, 81, 82, 83, 85, 86, 87, 89, 92, 97, 104, 116, 120
foreclosure, 95
funds, 45, 59, 71, 77, 80, 81, 103, 108, 109, 117, 118

G

Goliath, 5, 7, 8, 15, 17, 24, 140

government, 16, 86

Grisham, John, 41, 74

I

income, 15, 38, 39, 44, 47, 90, 98, 103, 109, 121, 122

injury, 15, 17, 27, 41, 51, 55, 120, 131

insurance, 15, 17, 24, 28, 29, 32, 38, 39, 40, 44, 72, 122

interest, 8, 31, 32, 39, 40, 45, 46, 47, 56, 57, 59, 60, 61, 64, 65,
    71, 72, 73, 74, 75, 76, 77, 79, 81, 82, 83, 86, 87, 88, 89, 90, 92,
    93, 94, 95, 97, 100, 101, 102, 105, 107, 108, 109, 110, 113, 114,
    115, 116, 118, 122, 124, 125

investment, 68, 93, 103, 127

IRC, 37, 108

IRS, 37, 38, 39, 41, 47, 108

J

jurisdictions, 37

L

lawsuits, 36

leases, 33, 125

lenders, 29, 35, 40, 47, 65, 77, 78, 80, 83, 108, 109, 110, 113, 114,
    116, 117, 118, 122, 125

lending, 40, 64, 72, 78, 79, 86, 92, 104, 109, 113, 114, 119

Liens, 124

liquidity, 73, 75, 78, 99, 121

loans, 37, 38, 39, 43, 47, 73, 78, 79, 80, 82, 83, 88, 105, 114, 116, 117, 122, 125

M

malpractice, 32, 55, 99

manufacturer, 34, 92, 102, 103

marketing, 28, 74, 82, 128

marketplace, 24, 71, 73, 98, 101, 109, 117, 122, 126, 127

medical, 23, 24, 32, 37, 98, 99

MRI, 23

N

negligence, 15

Neurology, 23

non-lawyers, 11, 17, 40

non-recourse, 56, 59, 60, 69

O

obligor, 72

out-lawyer, 65

P

PART, 13, 19, 49, 111

partner, 9, 31, 89, 92, 93, 95, 96, 123, 127

Pass-through, 53

payables, 86, 97

payments, 57, 73, 81, 82, 88, 91, 95, 97, 98, 99, 105, 115, 116, 127

payout, 63, 64

personal-injury, 17, 27, 41

pittance, 28

plaintiffs, 32, 89

PLR, 37

portfolio, 29, 40, 83, 90

Pre-payment, 116

price, 61, 63, 94, 100, 126

profits, 16, 61, 63, 89, 91, 92, 94, 100, 105, 116, 122, 126

protocols, 109

Q

quadriplegia, 22, 23

QuickBooks, 52

R

receivables, 28, 34, 44

reconciling, 92

recourse, 35, 56, 59, 60, 64, 69

reimbursements, 56

rent, 32, 37, 44, 81

retirement, 32

risk, 11, 36, 38, 42, 53, 56, 59, 64, 68, 69, 72, 79, 95, 101, 102, 110, 119

S

Schlichtmann, 41

self-funding, 90

services, 8, 17, 23, 36, 38, 45, 58, 59, 97, 98, 103, 114, 118, 124 settlement, 28, 58, 71, 72, 73, 74, 75, 76, 108

settlement-funding, 75

small-business, 92

statements, 47, 56, 92, 121, 127, 128, 129

Stoll, 23, 24

T

tax, 8, 27, 31, 38, 39, 41, 45, 46, 68, 83, 89, 90, 91, 92, 93, 95, 108, 109

tax-deductible, 83

time-consuming, 80

U

UCC, 46, 47, 64, 72, 125

underwriting, 56, 64, 68, 72, 78, 79, 95, 100, 101, 104, 114

V

valuation, 127

vehicles, 35

verdict, 67, 68

W

websites, 30, 113, 118, 127

witnesses, 24, 97, 107, 120

Z

zero-collateral, 86

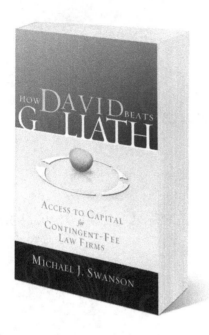

How can you use this book?

MOTIVATE

EDUCATE

THANK

INSPIRE

PROMOTE

CONNECT

Why have a custom version of *How David Beats Goliath*?

- Build personal bonds with customers, prospects, employees, donors, and key constituencies
- Develop a long-lasting reminder of your event, milestone, or celebration
- Provide a keepsake that inspires change in behavior and change in lives
- Deliver the ultimate "thank you" gift that remains on coffee tables and bookshelves
- Generate the "wow" factor

Books are thoughtful gifts that provide a genuine sentiment that other promotional items cannot express. They promote employee discussions and interaction, reinforce an event's meaning or location, and they make a lasting impression. Use your book to say "Thank You" and show people that you care.

How David Beats Goliath is available in bulk quantities and in customized versions at special discounts for corporate, institutional, and educational purposes. To learn more please contact our Special Sales team at:

1.866.775.1696 • sales@advantageww.com • www.AdvantageSpecialSales.com